# Elizabethan Sonnet Cycles

*Michael Drayton,
Bartholomew Griffin, and
William Smith*

# Contents

IDEA by MICHAEL DRAYTON ................................................................7
FIDESSA MORE CHASTE THAN KIND by B. GRIFFIN, GENT.............50
CHLORIS OR, THE COMPLAINT OF THE PASSIONATE ........................
DESPISED SHEPHERD by WILLIAM SMITH ...........................................87

# ELIZABETHAN SONNET CYCLES

BY

Michael Drayton, Bartholomew Griffin,
and William Smith

# IDEA
## by
# MICHAEL DRAYTON

The true story of the life of Michael Drayton might be told to vindicate the poetic traditions of the olden time. A child-poet wandering in fay-haunted Arden, or listening to the harper that frequented the fireside of Polesworth Hall where the boy was a petted page, later the honoured almoner of the bounty of many patrons, one who "not unworthily," as Tofte said, "beareth the name of the chiefest archangel, singing after this soule-ravishing manner," yet leaving but "five pounds lying by him at his death, which was satis viatici ad coelum"--is not this the panorama of a poetic career? But above all, to complete the picture of the ideal poet, he worshipped, and hopelessly, from youth to age the image of one, woman. He never married, and while many patronesses were honoured with his poetic addresses, there was one fair dame to whom he never offered dedicatory sonnet, a silence that is full of meaning. Yet the praises of Idea, his poetic name for the lady of his admiration and love, are written all over the pages of his voluminous lyrical and chorographical and historical poems, and her very name is quaintly revealed to us. Anne Goodere was the younger daughter in the noble family where Drayton was bred and educated; and one may picture the fair child standing "gravely merry" by the little page to listen to "John Hews his lyre," at that ancestral fireside. "Where I love, I love for years," said

Drayton in 1621. As late as 1627, but four years before his death, he writes an elegy of his lady's not coming to London, in which he complains that he has been starved for her short letters and has had to read last year's over again. About the same time he is writing that immortal sonnet, the sixty-first, the one that Rossetti, with perhaps something too much of partiality, has declared to be almost, if not quite, the best in the language. The tragedy of a whole life is concentrated in that sonnet, and the heart-pang in it is unmistakable. But Drayton had stood as witness to the will of Anne's father, by which L1500 was set down for her marriage portion. She was an heiress, he a penniless poet, and what was to be done?

About 1590, when Drayton was twenty-eight, and Anne was probably twenty-one years old, Drayton left Polesworth Hall and came to London. Perhaps the very parting was the means of revealing his heart to himself, for it is from near this time that, as he confesses later, he dates the first consciousness of his love. He soon publishes Idea, the Shepherd's Garland, Rowland's Sacrifice to the Nine Muses, where we first see our poet, in his pastoral-poetic character, carving his "rime of love's idolatry," upon a beechen tree. Thirteen stanzas of these pastoral eclogues do not exhaust the catalogue of her beauties; and when he praises the proportion of her shape and carriage, we know that it was not the poet's frenzied eye alone that saw these graces, for Dr. John Hall, of Stratford, who attended her professionally, records in his case-book that she was "beautiful and of gallant structure of body." Anne was married about 1595 to Sir Henry Rainsford, who became Drayton's friend, host and patron. It is likely that Lady Rainsford deserved a goodly portion of the praises bestowed upon her beauty. And she need not have been ashamed of the devotion of her knight of poesy; for Michael Drayton was, like Constable and Daniel and Fletcher, a man good and true, and the chorus of contemporaries that praise his character and his verse is led by pious Meres himself, and echoed by Jonson.

Idea's Mirrour, Amours in Quatorzains, formed the title under which the sonnet-cycle appeared in 1594. Idea was reprinted eight times before 1637, the edition of 1619 being the chief and serving for the foundation of our text. Many changes and additions were made by the author in the successive editions; in fact only twenty of the fifty-one "amours" in Idea's Mirrour escaped the winnowing, while the famous sixty-first appears for the first time in 1619. There is a distinct progress manifest in the subdual of language and form to artistic finish, and while the cycle in its unevenness represents the early and late stages of poetic progress, the more delicate examples of his work show him worthy of the praise bestowed by his latest admirer and critic,

> "Faith, Michael Drayton bears the bell
> For numbers airy."

It will be noted that, while many rhyme-arrangements are experimented upon, the Shakespearean or quatrain-and-couplet form predominates. In the less praiseworthy sonnets he is found to lack grammatical clamping and to allow frequent faults in rhythm, and he toys with the glittering and soulless conceit as much as any; but where his individuality has fullest sway, as in the picturesque Arden memory of the fifty-third, the personal reminiscences of the Ankor sonnets, and the vivid theatre theme of the forty-seventh, in what Main calls that "magical realisation of the spirit of evening" in the thirty-seventh, and above all in the naive and passionate sixty-first, there is a rude strength that pierces beneath the formalities and touches and moves the heart. Drayton, like Sidney and Daniel and Shakespeare, draws freely upon the general thought-storehouse of the Italianate sonneteers: time and the transitoriness of beauty, the lover's extremes, the Platonic ideas of soul-functions and of love-madness, the phoenix and Icarus and all the classic gods, engage his fancy first or last; and no sonnet trifler has been more attracted by the great theme of immortality in verse than he. When honouring Idea in the favourite mode he cries

> "Queens hereafter shall be glad to live
> Upon the alms of thy superfluous praise."

A late writer holds that years have falsified this prophecy. It is true that Lamb valued Drayton chiefly as the panegyrist of his native earth, and we would hardly venture to predict the future of our sonneteer; but the fact remains that now three hundred years after his time, his lifelong devotion to the prototype of Idea constitutes, as he conventionally asserted it would, his most valid claim to interest, and that the sonnets where this love has found most potent expression mount the nearest to the true note of immortality.

## TO THE READER OF THESE SONNETS

Into these loves who but for passion looks,
At this first sight here let him lay them by,
And seek elsewhere in turning other books,
Which better may his labour satisfy.
  No far-fetched sigh shall ever wound my breast;
Love from mine eye a tear shall never wring;
Nor in "Ah me's!" my whining sonnets drest,
A libertine fantasticly I sing.
  My verse is the true image of my mind,
Ever in motion, still desiring change;
To choice of all variety inclined,
And in all humours sportively I range.
  My muse is rightly of the English strain,
  That cannot long one fashion entertain.

# IDEA

I

Like an adventurous sea-farer am I,
Who hath some long and dang'rous voyage been,
And called to tell of his discovery,
How far he sailed, what countries he had seen,
  Proceeding from the port whence he put forth,
Shows by his compass how his course he steered,
When east, when west, when south, and when by north,
As how the pole to every place was reared,
  What capes he doubled, of what continent,
The gulfs and straits that strangely he had past,
Where most becalmed, where with foul weather spent,
And on what rocks in peril to be cast:
  Thus in my love, time calls me to relate
  My tedious travels and oft-varying fate.


II

My heart was slain, and none but you and I;
Who should I think the murder should commit?
Since but yourself there was no creature by
But only I, guiltless of murdering it.
  It slew itself; the verdict on the view

Do quit the dead, and me not accessary.
Well, well, I fear it will be proved by you,
The evidence so great a proof doth carry.
  But O see, see, we need inquire no further!
Upon your lips the scarlet drops are found,
And in your eye the boy that did the murder,
Your cheeks yet pale since first he gave the wound!
    By this I see, however things be past,
    Yet heaven will still have murder out at last.


### III

Taking my pen, with words to cast my woe,
Duly to count the sum of all my cares,
I find my griefs innumerable grow,
The reck'nings rise to millions of despairs.
  And thus dividing of my fatal hours,
The payments of my love I read and cross;
Subtracting, set my sweets unto my sours,
My joys' arrearage leads me to my loss.
  And thus mine eyes a debtor to thine eye,
Which by extortion gaineth all their looks,
My heart hath paid such grievous usury,
That all their wealth lies in thy beauty's books.
    And all is thine which hath been due to me,
    And I a bankrupt, quite undone by thee.

IV

Bright star of beauty, on whose eyelids sit
A thousand nymph-like and enamoured graces,
The goddesses of memory and wit,
Which there in order take their several places;
  In whose dear bosom, sweet delicious love
Lays down his quiver which he once did bear,
Since he that blessed paradise did prove,
And leaves his mother's lap to sport him there
  Let others strive to entertain with words
My soul is of a braver mettle made;
I hold that vile which vulgar wit affords;
In me's that faith which time cannot invade.
  Let what I praise be still made good by you;
  Be you most worthy whilst I am most true!


V

Nothing but "No!" and "I!"[A] and "I!" and "No!"
"How falls it out so strangely?" you reply.
I tell ye, Fair, I'll not be answered so,
With this affirming "No!" denying "I!"
I say "I love!" You slightly answer "I!"
I say "You love!" You pule me out a "No!"
I say "I die!" You echo me with "I!"
"Save me!" I cry; you sigh me out a "No!"
Must woe and I have naught but "No!" and "I!"?
No "I!" am I, if I no more can have.
Answer no more; with silence make reply,
And let me take myself what I do crave;

Let "No!" and "I!" with I and you be so,
Then answer "No!" and "I!" and "I!" and "No!"

[Footnote A: The "I" of course equals "aye."]


VI

How many paltry, foolish, painted things,
That now in coaches trouble every street,
Shall be forgotten, whom no poet sings,
Ere they be well wrapped in their winding sheet!
  Where I to thee eternity shall give,
When nothing else remaineth of these days,
And queens hereafter shall be glad to live
Upon the alms of thy superfluous praise;
  Virgins and matrons reading these my rhymes,
Shall be so much delighted with thy story,
That they shall grieve they lived not in these times,
To have seen thee, their sex's only glory.
  So shalt thou fly above the vulgar throng,
  Still to survive in my immortal song.


VII

Love, in a humour, played the prodigal,
And bade my senses to a solemn feast;
Yet more to grace the company withal,
Invites my heart to be the chiefest guest.
  No other drink would serve this glutton's turn,
But precious tears distilling from mine eyne,
Which with my sighs this epicure doth burn,

Quaffing carouses in this costly wine;
  Where, in his cups, o'ercome with foul excess,
Straightways he plays a swaggering ruffian's part,
And at the banquet in his drunkenness,
Slew his dear friend, my kind and truest heart.
  A gentle warning, friends, thus may you see,
  What 'tis to keep a drunkard company!


## VIII

There's nothing grieves me but that age should haste,
That in my days I may not see thee old;
That where those two clear sparkling eyes are placed,
Only two loopholes that I might behold;
  That lovely arched ivory-polished brow
Defaced with wrinkles, that I might but see;
Thy dainty hair, so curled and crisped now,
Like grizzled moss upon some aged tree;
  Thy cheek now flush with roses, sunk and lean;
Thy lips, with age as any wafer thin!
Thy pearly teeth out of thy head so clean,
That when thou feed'st thy nose shall touch thy chin!
  These lines that now thou scornst, which should delight thee,
  Then would I make thee read but to despite thee.


## IX

As other men, so I myself do muse
Why in this sort I wrest invention so,
And why these giddy metaphors I use,
Leaving the path the greater part do go.

I will resolve you. I'm a lunatic;
And ever this in madmen you shall find,
What they last thought of when the brain grew sick,
In most distraction they keep that in mind.
  Thus talking idly in this bedlam fit,
Reason and I, you must conceive, are twain;
'Tis nine years now since first I lost my wit.
Bear with me then though troubled be my brain.
  With diet and correction men distraught,
  Not too far past, may to their wits be brought.


X

To nothing fitter can I thee compare
Than to the son of some rich penny-father,
Who having now brought on his end with care,
Leaves to his son all he had heaped together.
  This new rich novice, lavish of his chest,
To one man gives, doth on another spend;
Then here he riots; yet amongst the rest,
Haps to lend some to one true honest friend.
  Thy gifts thou in obscurity dost waste:
False friends, thy kindness born but to deceive thee;
Thy love that is on the unworthy placed;
Time hath thy beauty which with age will leave thee.
  Only that little which to me was lent,
  I give thee back when all the rest is spent.

XI

You're not alone when you are still alone;
O God! from you that I could private be!
Since you one were, I never since was one;
Since you in me, myself since out of me.
  Transported from myself into your being,
Though either distant, present yet to either;
Senseless with too much joy, each other seeing;
And only absent when we are together.
  Give me my self, and take your self again!
Devise some means but how I may forsake you!
So much is mine that doth with you remain,
That taking what is mine, with me I take you.
  You do bewitch me! O that I could fly
  From my self you, or from your own self I!

## TO THE SOUL

XII

That learned Father which so firmly proves
The soul of man immortal and divine,
And doth the several offices define

| | |
|---|---|
| Anima. | Gives her that name, as she the body moves. |
| Amor. | Then is she love, embracing charity. |
| Animus. | Moving a will in us, it is the mind; |
| Mens. | Retaining knowledge, still the same in kind. |
| Memoria. | As intellectual, it is memory. |
| Ratio. | In judging, reason only is her name. |
| Sensus. | In speedy apprehension, it is sense. |

Conscientia.  In right and wrong they call her conscience;
Spiritus.     The spirit, when it to God-ward doth inflame:
These of the soul the several functions be,
Which my heart lightened by thy love doth see.

# TO THE SHADOW

XIII

Letters and lines we see are soon defaced
  Metals do waste and fret with canker's rust,
  The diamond shall once consume to dust,
And freshest colours with foul stains disgraced;
Paper and ink can paint but naked words,
  To write with blood of force offends the sight;
  And if with tears, I find them all too light,
And sighs and signs a silly hope affords.
O sweetest shadow, how thou serv'st my turn!
  Which still shalt be as long as there is sun,
  Nor whilst the world is never shall be done;
Whilst moon shall shine or any fire shall burn,
  That everything whence shadow doth proceed,
  May in his shadow my love's story read.


XIV

If he, from heaven that filched that living fire,
  Condemned by Jove to endless torment be,
  I greatly marvel how you still go free
That far beyond Prometheus did aspire.
The fire he stole, although of heavenly kind,

   Which from above he craftily did take,
     Of lifeless clods us living men to make
He did bestow in temper of the mind.
But you broke into heaven's immortal store,
   Where virtue, honour, wit, and beauty lay;
   Which taking thence, you have escaped away,
Yet stand as free as e'er you did before.
   Yet old Prometheus punished for his rape;
   Thus poor thieves suffer when the greater 'scape.

# HIS REMEDY FOR LOVE

## XV

Since to obtain thee nothing me will stead,
I have a med'cine that shall cure my love.
The powder of her heart dried, when she's dead,
That gold nor honour ne'er had power to move;
  Mixed with her tears that ne'er her true love crost,
Nor at fifteen ne'er longed to be a bride;
Boiled with her sighs, in giving up the ghost,
That for her late deceased husband died;
  Into the same then let a woman breathe,
That being chid did never word reply;
With one thrice married's prayers, that did bequeath
A legacy to stale virginity.
  If this receipt have not the power to win me,
  Little I'll say, but think the devil's in me!

## AN ALLUSION TO THE PHOENIX

XVI

'Mongst all the creatures in this spacious round
  Of the birds' kind, the phoenix is alone,
  Which best by you of living things is known;
None like to that, none like to you is found!
Your beauty is the hot and splend'rous sun;
  The precious spices be your chaste desire,
  Which being kindled by that heavenly fire,
Your life, so like the phoenix's begun.
Yourself thus burned in that sacred flame,
  With so rare sweetness all the heavens perfuming;
  Again increasing as you are consuming,
Only by dying born the very same.
  And winged by fame you to the stars ascend;
  So you of time shall live beyond the end.

## TO TIME

XVII

Stay, speedy time! Behold, before thou pass
  From age to age, what thou hast sought to see,
  One in whom all the excellencies be,
In whom heaven looks itself as in a glass.
Time, look thou too in this translucent glass,
  And thy youth past in this pure mirror see!
  As the world's beauty in his infancy,

What it was then, and thou before it was.
Pass on and to posterity tell this--
  Yet see thou tell but truly what hath been.
  Say to our nephews that thou once hast seen
In perfect human shape all heavenly bliss;
  And bid them mourn, nay more, despair with thee,
  That she is gone, her like again to see.


# TO THE CELESTIAL NUMBERS

### XVIII

To this our world, to learning, and to heaven,
  Three nines there are, to every one a nine;
  One number of the earth, the other both divine;
One woman now makes three odd numbers even.
Nine orders first of angels be in heaven;
  Nine muses do with learning still frequent:
  These with the gods are ever resident.
Nine worthy women to the world were given.
My worthy one to these nine worthies addeth;
  And my fair Muse, one Muse unto the nine.
  And my good angel, in my soul divine!--
With one more order these nine orders gladdeth.
  My Muse, my worthy, and my angel then
  Makes every one of these three nines a ten.

# TO HUMOUR

### XIX

You cannot love, my pretty heart, and why?
There was a time you told me that you would,
But how again you will the same deny.
If it might please you, would to God you could!
  What, will you hate? Nay, that you will not neither;
  Nor love, nor hate! How then? What will you do?
What, will you keep a mean then betwixt either?
Or will you love me, and yet hate me too?
  Yet serves not this! What next, what other shift?
You will, and will not; what a coil is here!
I see your craft, now I perceive your drift,
And all this while I was mistaken there.
  Your love and hate is this, I now do prove you:
  You love in hate, by hate to make me love you.


### XX

An evil spirit, your beauty, haunts me still,
Wherewith, alas, I have been long possessed!
Which ceaseth not to tempt me to each ill,
Nor give me once but one poor minute's rest.
  In me it speaks whether I sleep or wake;
And when by means to drive it out I try,
With greater torments then it me doth take,
And tortures me in most extremity.
  Before my face it lays down my despairs,
And hastes me on unto a sudden death;

Now tempting me to drown myself in tears,
And then in sighing to give up my breath.
  Thus am I still provoked to every evil,
    By this good wicked spirit, sweet angel-devil.


## XXI

A witless gallant a young wench that wooed--
Yet his dull spirit her not one jot could move--
Intreated me as e'er I wished his good,
To write him but one sonnet to his love.
  When I as fast as e'er my pen could trot,
Poured out what first from quick invention came,
Nor never stood one word thereof to blot;
Much like his wit that was to use the same.
  But with my verses he his mistress won,
Who doated on the dolt beyond all measure.
But see, for you to heaven for phrase I run,
And ransack all Apollo's golden treasure!
  Yet by my troth, this fool his love obtains,
    And I lose you for all my wit and pains!


# TO FOLLY

## XXII

With fools and children good discretion bears;
  Then, honest people, bear with love and me,
  Nor older yet nor wiser made by years,
Amongst the rest of fools and children be.
  Love, still a baby, plays with gauds and toys,

And like a wanton sports with every feather,
And idiots still are running after boys;
Then fools and children fitt'st to go together.
  He still as young as when he first was born,
Nor wiser I than when as young as he;
You that behold us, laugh us not to scorn;
Give nature thanks you are not such as we!
    Yet fools and children sometimes tell in play;
    Some wise in show, more fools indeed than they.


## XXIII

Love, banished heaven, in earth was held in scorn,
Wand'ring abroad in need and beggary;
And wanting friends, though of a goddess born,
Yet craved the alms of such as passed by.
  I, like a man devout and charitable,
Clothed the naked, lodged this wandering guest;
With sighs and tears still furnishing his table
With what might make the miserable blest.
  But this ungrateful for my good desert,
Enticed my thoughts against me to conspire,
Who gave consent to steal away my heart,
And set my breast, his lodging, on a fire.
    Well, well, my friends, when beggars grow thus bold,
    No marvel then though charity grow cold.

## XXIV

I hear some say, "This man is not in love!"
"Who! can he love? a likely thing!" they say.
"Read but his verse, and it will easily prove!"
O, judge not rashly, gentle Sir, I pray!
  Because I loosely trifle in this sort,
As one that fain his sorrows would beguile,
You now suppose me all this time in sport,
And please yourself with this conceit the while.
  Ye shallow cens'rers! sometimes, see ye not,
In greatest perils some men pleasant be,
Where fame by death is only to be got,
They resolute! So stands the case with me.
  Where other men in depth of passion cry,
  I laugh at fortune, as in jest to die.


## XXV

O, why should nature niggardly restrain
That foreign nations relish not our tongue?
Else should my lines glide on the waves of Rhine,
And crown the Pyren's with my living song.
  But bounded thus, to Scotland get you forth!
Thence take you wing unto the Orcades!
There let my verse get glory in the north,
Making my sighs to thaw the frozen seas.
  And let the bards within that Irish isle,
To whom my Muse with fiery wings shall pass,
Call back the stiff-necked rebels from exile,
And mollify the slaughtering gallowglass;

And when my flowing numbers they rehearse,
Let wolves and bears be charmed with my verse.

# TO DESPAIR

XXVI

I ever love where never hope appears,
  Yet hope draws on my never-hoping care,
  And my life's hope would die but for despair;
My never certain joy breeds ever certain fears.
Uncertain dread gives wings unto my hope;
  Yet my hope's wings are laden so with fear
  As they cannot ascend to my hope's sphere,
Though fear gives them more than a heavenly scope.
Yet this large room is bounded with despair,
  So my love is still fettered with vain hope,
  And liberty deprives him of his scope,
And thus am I imprisoned in the air.
  Then, sweet despair, awhile hold up thy head,
  Or all my hope for sorrow will be dead.

XXVII

Is not love here as 'tis in other climes,
And differeth it as do the several nations?
Or hath it lost the virtue with the times,
Or in this island alt'reth with the fashions?
  Or have our passions lesser power than theirs,
Who had less art them lively to express?
Is nature grown less powerful in their heirs,

Or in our fathers did she more transgress?
  I am sure my sighs come from a heart as true
As any man's that memory can boast,
And my respects and services to you,
Equal with his that loves his mistress most.
  Or nature must be partial in my cause,
  Or only you do violate her laws.


XXVIII

To such as say thy love I overprize,
And do not stick to term my praises folly,
Against these folks that think themselves so wise,
I thus oppose my reason's forces wholly:
  Though I give more than well affords my state,
In which expense the most suppose me vain
Which yields them nothing at the easiest rate,
Yet at this price returns me treble gain;
  They value not, unskilful how to use,
And I give much because I gain thereby.
I that thus take or they that thus refuse,
Whether are these deceived then, or I?
  In everything I hold this maxim still,
  The circumstance doth make it good or ill.

## TO THE SENSES

XXIX

When conquering love did first my heart assail,
Unto mine aid I summoned every sense,
Doubting if that proud tyrant should prevail,
My heart should suffer for mine eyes' offence.
  But he with beauty first corrupted sight,
My hearing bribed with her tongue's harmony,
My taste by her sweet lips drawn with delight,
My smelling won with her breath's spicery,
  But when my touching came to play his part,
The king of senses, greater than the rest,
He yields love up the keys unto my heart,
And tells the others how they should be blest.
  And thus by those of whom I hoped for aid,
  To cruel love my soul was first betrayed.

## TO THE VESTALS

XXX

Those priests which first the vestal fire begun,
Which might be borrowed from no earthly flame,
Devised a vessel to receive the sun,
Being stedfastly opposed to the same;
  Where with sweet wood laid curiously by art,
On which the sun might by reflection beat,
Receiving strength for every secret part,

The fuel kindled with celestial heat.
  Thy blessed eyes, the sun which lights this fire,
My holy thoughts, they be the vestal flame,
Thy precious odours be my chaste desires,
My breast's the vessel which includes the same;
  Thou art my Vesta, thou my goddess art,
  Thy hallowed temple only is my heart.

# TO THE CRITICS

### XXXI

Methinks I see some crooked mimic jeer,
And tax my Muse with this fantastic grace;
Turning my papers asks, "What have we here?"
Making withal some filthy antic face.
  I fear no censure nor what thou canst say,
Nor shall my spirit one jot of vigour lose.
Think'st thou, my wit shall keep the packhorse way,
That every dudgeon low invention goes?
  Since sonnets thus in bundles are imprest,
And every drudge doth dull our satiate ear,
Think'st thou my love shall in those rags be drest
That every dowdy, every trull doth wear?
  Up to my pitch no common judgment flies;
  I scorn all earthly dung-bred scarabies.

## TO THE RIVER ANKOR

XXXII

Our floods' queen, Thames, for ships and swans is crowned,
And stately Severn for her shore is praised;
The crystal Trent for fords and fish renowned,
And Avon's fame to Albion's cliff is raised.
  Carlegion Chester vaunts her holy Dee;
York many wonders of her Ouse can tell;
The Peak, her Dove, whose banks so fertile be;
And Kent will say her Medway doth excel.
  Cotswold commends her Isis to the Thame;
Our northern borders boast of Tweed's fair flood;
Our western parts extol their Wilis' fame;
And the old Lea brags of the Danish blood.
  Arden's sweet Ankor, let thy glory be,
  That fair Idea only lives by thee!

## TO IMAGINATION

XXXIII

Whilst yet mine eyes do surfeit with delight,
My woful heart imprisoned in my breast,
Wisheth to be transformed to my sight,
That it like those by looking might be blest.
  But whilst mine eyes thus greedily do gaze,
Finding their objects over-soon depart,
These now the other's happiness do praise,

Wishing themselves that they had been my heart,
  That eyes were heart, or that the heart were eyes,
As covetous the other's use to have.
But finding nature their request denies,
This to each other mutually they crave;
  That since the one cannot the other be,
  That eyes could think of that my heart could see.

## TO ADMIRATION

XXXIV

Marvel not, love, though I thy power admire,
  Ravished a world beyond the farthest thought,
  And knowing more than ever hath been taught,
That I am only starved in my desire.
Marvel not, love, though I thy power admire,
  Aiming at things exceeding all perfection,
  To wisdom's self to minister direction,
That I am only starved in my desire.
Marvel not, love, though I thy power admire,
  Though my conceit I further seem to bend
  Than possibly invention can extend,
And yet am only starved in my desire.
  If thou wilt wonder, here's the wonder, love,
  That this to me doth yet no wonder prove.

## TO MIRACLE

XXXV

Some misbelieving and profane in love,
  When I do speak of miracles by thee,
  May say that thou art flattered by me,
Who only write my skill in verse to prove
See miracles, ye unbelieving, see!
  A dumb-born Muse made to express the mind,
  A cripple hand to write, yet lame by kind,
One by thy name, the other touching thee.
Blind were mine eyes, till they were seen of thine;
  And mine ears deaf by thy fame healed be;
  My vices cured by virtues sprung from thee;
My hopes revived which long in grave had lien.
  All unclean thoughts, foul spirits, cast out in me,
  Only by virtue that proceeds from thee.

## CUPID CONJURED

XXXVI

Thou purblind boy, since thou hast been so slack
To wound her heart whose eyes have wounded me
And suffered her to glory in my wrack,
Thus to my aid I lastly conjure thee!
  By hellish Styx, by which the Thund'rer swears,
By thy fair mother's unavoided power,

By Hecate's names, by Proserpine's sad tears,
When she was wrapt to the infernal bower!
  By thine own loved Psyche, by the fires
Spent on thine altars flaming up to heaven,
By all true lovers' sighs, vows, and desires,
By all the wounds that ever thou hast given;
  I conjure thee by all that I have named,
  To make her love, or, Cupid, be thou damned!


XXXVII

Dear, why should you command me to my rest,
When now the night doth summon all to sleep?
Methinks this time becometh lovers best;
Night was ordained together friends to keep.
  How happy are all other living things,
Which though the day disjoin by several flight,
The quiet evening yet together brings,
And each returns unto his love at night!
  O thou that art so courteous else to all,
Why shouldst thou, Night, abuse me only thus,
That every creature to his kind dost call,
And yet 'tis thou dost only sever us?
  Well could I wish it would be ever day,
  If when night comes, you bid me go away.


XXXVIII

Sitting alone, love bids me go and write;
  Reason plucks back, commanding me to stay,
  Boasting that she doth still direct the way,

Or else love were unable to indite.
Love growing angry, vexed at the spleen,
  And scorning reason's maimed argument,
  Straight taxeth reason, wanting to invent
Where she with love conversing hath not been.
Reason reproached with this coy disdain,
  Despiteth love, and laugheth at her folly;
  And love contemning reason's reason wholly,
Thought it in weight too light by many a grain.
  Reason put back doth out of sight remove,
  And love alone picks reason out of love.

## XXXIX

Some, when in rhyme they of their loves do tell,
With flames and lightnings their exordiums paint.
Some call on heaven, some invocate on hell,
And Fates and Furies, with their woes acquaint.
  Elizium is too high a seat for me,
I will not come in Styx or Phlegethon,
The thrice-three Muses but too wanton be,
Like they that lust, I care not, I will none.
  Spiteful Erinnys frights me with her looks,
My manhood dares not with foul Ate mell,
I quake to look on Hecate's charming books,
I still fear bugbears in Apollo's cell.
  I pass not for Minerva, nor Astrea,
  Only I call on my divine Idea!

XL

My heart the anvil where my thoughts do beat,
My words the hammers fashioning my desire,
My breast the forge including all the heat,
Love is the fuel which maintains the fire;
  My sighs the bellows which the flame increaseth,
Filling mine ears with noise and nightly groaning;
Toiling with pain, my labour never ceaseth,
In grievous passions my woes still bemoaning;
  My eyes with tears against the fire striving,
Whose scorching gleed my heart to cinders turneth;
But with those drops the flame again reviving,
Still more and more it to my torment burneth,
  With Sisyphus thus do I roll the stone,
  And turn the wheel with damned Ixion.

# LOVE'S LUNACY

XLI

Why do I speak of joy or write of love,
When my heart is the very den of horror,
And in my soul the pains of hell I prove,
With all his torments and infernal terror?
  What should I say? what yet remains to do?
My brain is dry with weeping all too long;
My sighs be spent in utt'ring of my woe,
And I want words wherewith to tell my wrong.
  But still distracted in love's lunacy,
And bedlam-like thus raving in my grief,

Now rail upon her hair, then on her eye,
Now call her goddess, then I call her thief;
  Now I deny her, then I do confess her,
  Now do I curse her, then again I bless her.


XLII

Some men there be which like my method well,
  And much commend the strangeness of my vein;
  Some say I have a passing pleasing strain,
Some say that in my humour I excel.
Some who not kindly relish my conceit,
  They say, as poets do, I use to feign,
  And in bare words paint out by passions' pain.
Thus sundry men their sundry minds repeat.
I pass not, I, how men affected be,
  Nor who commends or discommends my verse!
  It pleaseth me if I my woes rehearse,
And in my lines if she my love may see.
  Only my comfort still consists in this,
  Writing her praise I cannot write amiss.


XLIII

Why should your fair eyes with such sov'reign grace
Disperse their rays on every vulgar spirit,
Whilst I in darkness in the self-same place,
Get not one glance to recompense my merit?
  So doth the plowman gaze the wand'ring star,
  And only rest contented with the light,
That never learned what constellations are,

Beyond the bent of his unknowing sight.
  O why should beauty, custom to obey,
To their gross sense apply herself so ill!
Would God I were as ignorant as they,
When I am made unhappy by my skill,
  Only compelled on this poor good to boast!
  Heavens are not kind to them that know them most.


## XLIV

Whilst thus my pen strives to eternise thee,
Age rules my lines with wrinkles in my face,
Where in the map of all my misery
Is modelled out the world of my disgrace;
  Whilst in despite of tyrannising times,
Medea-like, I make thee young again,
Proudly thou scorn'st my world-outwearing rhymes,
And murther'st virtue with thy coy disdain;
  And though in youth my youth untimely perish,
To keep thee from oblivion and the grave,
Ensuing ages yet my rhymes shall cherish,
Where I intombed my better part shall save;
  And though this earthly body fade and die,
  My name shall mount upon eternity.


## XLV

Muses which sadly sit about my chair,
Drowned in the tears extorted by my lines;
With heavy sighs whilst thus I break the air,
Painting my passions in these sad designs,

Since she disdains to bless my happy verse,
The strong built trophies to her living fame,
Ever henceforth my bosom be your hearse,
Wherein the world shall now entomb her name.
  Enclose my music, you poor senseless walls,
Sith she is deaf and will not hear my moans;
Soften yourselves with every tear that falls,
Whilst I like Orpheus sing to trees and stones,
  Which with my plaint seem yet with pity moved,
  Kinder than she whom I so long have loved.


### XLVI

Plain-pathed experience, the unlearned's guide,
Her simple followers evidently shows
Sometimes what schoolmen scarcely can decide,
Nor yet wise reason absolutely knows;
  In making trial of a murder wrought,
If the vile actors of the heinous deed
Near the dead body happily be brought,
Oft 't hath been proved the breathless corse will bleed.
  She coming near, that my poor heart hath slain,
Long since departed, to the world no more,
The ancient wounds no longer can contain,
But fall to bleeding as they did before.
  But what of this? Should she to death be led,
  It furthers justice but helps not the dead.

## XLVII

In pride of wit, when high desire of fame
Gave life and courage to my lab'ring pen,
And first the sound and virtue of my name
Won grace and credit in the ears of men,
  With those the thronged theatres that press,
I in the circuit for the laurel strove,
Where the full praise I freely must confess,
In heat of blood a modest mind might move;
  With shouts and claps at every little pause,
When the proud round on every side hath rung,
Sadly I sit unmoved with the applause,
As though to me it nothing did belong.
  No public glory vainly I pursue;
  All that I seek is to eternise you.


## XLVIII

Cupid, I hate thee, which I'd have thee know;
A naked starveling ever mayst thou be!
Poor rogue, go pawn thy fascia and thy bow
For some poor rags wherewith to cover thee;
  Or if thou'lt not thy archery forbear,
To some base rustic do thyself prefer,
And when corn's sown or grown into the ear,
Practice thy quiver and turn crowkeeper;
  Or being blind, as fittest for the trade,
Go hire thyself some bungling harper's boy;
They that are blind are minstrels often made,
So mayst thou live to thy fair mother's joy;

That whilst with Mars she holdeth her old way,
Thou, her blind son, mayst sit by them and play.


XLIX

Thou leaden brain, which censur'st what I write,
And sayst my lines be dull and do not move,
I marvel not thou feel'st not my delight,
Which never felt'st my fiery touch of love;
  But thou whose pen hath like a packhorse served,
Whose stomach unto gall hath turned thy food,
Whose senses like poor prisoners, hunger-starved
Whose grief hath parched thy body, dried thy blood;
  Thou which hast scorned life and hated death,
And in a moment, mad, sober, glad, and sorry;
Thou which hast banned thy thoughts and curst thy birth
With thousand plagues more than in purgatory;
  Thou thus whose spirit love in his fire refines,
  Come thou and read, admire, applaud my lines!


L

As in some countries far remote from hence,
The wretched creature destined to die,
Having the judgment due to his offence,
By surgeons begged, their art on him to try,
  Which on the living work without remorse,
First make incision on each mastering vein,
Then staunch the bleeding, then transpierce the corse,
And with their balms recure the wounds again,
  Then poison and with physic him restore;

Not that they fear the hopeless man to kill,
But their experience to increase the more:
Even so my mistress works upon my ill,
  By curing me and killing me each hour,
  Only to show her beauty's sovereign power.

## LI

Calling to mind since first my love begun,
Th'uncertain times, oft varying in their course,
How things still unexpectedly have run,
As't please the Fates by their resistless force;
  Lastly, mine eyes amazedly have seen
Essex's great fall, Tyrone his peace to gain,
The quiet end of that long living Queen,
This King's fair entrance, and our peace with Spain,
  We and the Dutch at length ourselves to sever;
Thus the world doth and evermore shall reel;
Yet to my goddess am I constant ever,
Howe'er blind Fortune turn her giddy wheel;
  Though heaven and earth prove both to me untrue,
  Yet am I still inviolate to you.

## LII

What dost thou mean to cheat me of my heart,
To take all mine and give me none again?
Or have thine eyes such magic or that art
That what they get they ever do retain?
  Play not the tyrant but take some remorse;
Rebate thy spleen if but for pity's sake;

Or cruel, if thou can'st not, let us scorse,
And for one piece of thine my whole heart take.
  But what of pity do I speak to thee,
Whose breast is proof against complaint or prayer?
Or can I think what my reward shall be
From that proud beauty which was my betrayer!
  What talk I of a heart when thou hast none?
  Or if thou hast, it is a flinty one.

# ANOTHER TO THE RIVER ANKOR

LIII

Clear Ankor, on whose silver-sanded shore,
My soul-shrined saint, my fair Idea lives;
O blessed brook, whose milk-white swans adore
Thy crystal stream, refined by her eyes,
  Where sweet myrrh-breathing Zephyr in the spring
Gently distils his nectar-dropping showers,
Where nightingales in Arden sit and sing
Amongst the dainty dew-impearled flowers;
  Say thus, fair brook, when thou shalt see thy queen,
"Lo, here thy shepherd spent his wand'ring years
And in these shades, dear nymph, he oft hath been;
And here to thee he sacrificed his tears."
  Fair Arden, thou my Tempe art alone,
  And thou, sweet Ankor, art my Helicon!

### LIV

Yet read at last the story of my woe,
The dreary abstracts of my endless cares,
With my life's sorrow interlined so,
Smoked with my sighs, and blotted with my tears,
  The sad memorials of my miseries,
Penned in the grief of mine afflicted ghost,
My life's complaint in doleful elegies,
With so pure love as time could never boast.
  Receive the incense which I offer here,
By my strong faith ascending to thy fame,
My zeal, my hope, my vows, my praise, my prayer,
My soul's oblations to thy sacred name;
  Which name my Muse to highest heavens shall raise,
By chaste desire, true love, and virtuous praise.


### LV

My fair, if thou wilt register my love,
A world of volumes shall thereof arise;
Preserve my tears, and thou thyself shall prove
A second flood down raining from mine eyes;
  Note but my sighs, and thine eyes shall behold
The sunbeams smothered with immortal smoke;
And if by thee my prayers may be enrolled,
They heaven and earth to pity shall provoke.
  Look thou into my breast, and thou shalt see
Chaste holy vows for my soul's sacrifice,
That soul, sweet maid, which so hath honoured thee,
Erecting trophies to thy sacred eyes,

Those eyes to my heart shining ever bright,
When darkness hath obscured each other light.

# AN ALLUSION TO THE EAGLETS

## LVI

When like an eaglet I first found my love,
For that the virtue I thereof would know,
Upon the nest I set it forth to prove
If it were of that kingly kind or no;
  But it no sooner saw my sun appear,
But on her rays with open eyes it stood,
To show that I had hatched it for the air,
And rightly came from that brave mounting brood;
  And when the plumes were summed with sweet desire,
To prove the pinions it ascends the skies;
Do what I could, it needsly would aspire
To my soul's sun, those two celestial eyes.
  Thus from my breast, where it was bred alone,
  It after thee is like an eaglet flown.

## LVII

You best discerned of my mind's inward eyes,
And yet your graces outwardly divine,
Whose dear remembrance in my bosom lies,
Too rich a relic for so poor a shrine;
  You, in whom nature chose herself to view,
When she her own perfection would admire;
Bestowing all her excellence on you,

At whose pure eyes Love lights his hallowed fire;
  Even as a man that in some trance hath seen
More than his wond'ring utterance can unfold,
That rapt in spirit in better worlds hath been,
So must your praise distractedly be told;
  Most of all short when I would show you most,
  In your perfections so much am I lost.


LVIII

In former times, such as had store of coin,
In wars at home or when for conquests bound,
For fear that some their treasure should purloin,
Gave it to keep to spirits within the ground;
  And to attend it them as strongly tied
Till they returned. Home when they never came,
Such as by art to get the same have tried,
From the strong spirit by no means force the same.
  Nearer men come, that further flies away,
Striving to hold it strongly in the deep.
Ev'n as this spirit, so you alone do play
With those rich beauties Heav'n gives you to keep;
  Pity so left to th' coldness of your blood,
  Not to avail you nor do others good.

# TO PROVERBS

### LIX

As Love and I late harboured in one inn,
With Proverbs thus each other entertain.
"In love there is no lack," thus I begin:
"Fair words make fools," replieth he again.
  "Who spares to speak, doth spare to speed," quoth I.
"As well," saith he, "too forward as too slow."
"Fortune assists the boldest," I reply.
"A hasty man," quoth he, "ne'er wanted woe!"
  "Labour is light, where love," quoth I, "doth pay."
Saith he, "Light burden's heavy, if far born."
Quoth I, "The main lost, cast the by away!"
  "You have spun a fair thread," he replies in scorn.
  And having thus awhile each other thwarted,
  Fools as we met, so fools again we parted.

### LX

Define my weal, and tell the joys of heaven;
Express my woes and show the pains of hell;
Declare what fate unlucky stars have given,
And ask a world upon my life to dwell;
  Make known the faith that fortune could no move,
Compare my worth with others' base desert,
Let virtue be the touchstone of my love,
So may the heavens read wonders in my heart;
  Behold the clouds which have eclipsed my sun,
And view the crosses which my course do let;

Tell me, if ever since the world begun
So fair a rising had so foul a set?
  And see if time, if he would strive to prove,
  Can show a second to so pure a love.


## LXI

Since there's no help, come let us kiss and part,
Nay I have done, you get no more of me;
And I am glad, yea glad with all my heart,
That thus so cleanly I myself can free;
  Shakes hands for ever, cancel all our vows,
And when we meet at any time again,
Be it not seen in either of our brows
That we one jot of former love retain.
  Now at the last gasp of Love's latest breath,
When his pulse failing, Passion speechless lies,
When Faith is kneeling by his bed of death,
And Innocence is closing up his eyes:
  Now if thou wouldst, when all have given him over,
  From death to life thou might'st him yet recover!


## LXII

When first I ended, then I first began;
Then more I travelled further from my rest.
Where most I lost, there most of all I won;
Pined with hunger, rising from a feast.
  Methinks I fly, yet want I legs to go,
Wise in conceit, in act a very sot,
Ravished with joy amidst a hell of woe,

What most I seem that surest am I not.
  I build my hopes a world above the sky,
Yet with the mole I creep into the earth;
In plenty I am starved with penury,
And yet I surfeit in the greatest dearth.
  I have, I want, despair, and yet desire,
    Burned in a sea of ice, and drowned amidst a fire.

### LXIII

Truce, gentle Love, a parley now I crave,
Methinks 'tis long since first these wars begun;
Nor thou, nor I, the better yet can have;
Bad is the match where neither party won.
  I offer free conditions of fair peace,
My heart for hostage that it shall remain.
Discharge our forces, here let malice cease,
So for my pledge thou give me pledge again.
  Or if no thing but death will serve thy turn,
Still thirsting for subversion of my state,
Do what thou canst, raze, massacre, and burn;
Let the world see the utmost of thy hate;
  I send defiance, since if overthrown,
    Thou vanquishing, the conquest is mine own.

# FIDESSA
# MORE CHASTE THAN KIND
# by
# B. GRIFFIN, GENT.

## BARTHOLOMEW GRIFFIN

The author of Fidessa has gained undeserved notice from the fact that the piratical printer W. Jaggard, included a transcript of one of his sonnets in a volume that he put forth in 1599, under the name of Shakespeare. It would be easy to believe, in spite of the doubtful rimes characteristic of Fidessa, that sonnet three was not Griffin's, for no singer in the Elizabethan choir was more skilful in turning his voice to other people's melodies than was he. He has been called "a gross plagiary;" yet it must be realised that the sonneteers of that time felt they had a right, almost a duty, to take up the poetic themes used by their models. Griffin shows great ingenuity in the manipulation of the stock-themes, and the lover of Petrarch and all the young Abraham-Slenders of the day must have been delighted with the familiar "designs" as they re-appeared in Fidessa.

Bartholomew Griffin was buried in Coventry in 1602. In 1596 he dedicated his "slender work" Fidessa to William Essex of Lamebourne in Berkshire. He adds an address to the Gentlemen of the Inns of Court, whom he begs to "censure mildly as protectors of a poor stranger" and "judge the best as encouragers of a young beginner." Of the poet little further is known. From the sonnets themselves we learn that Fidessa was "of high regard," the child of a beautiful mother and of a renowned father; she sprang in fact from the same root with the poet himself, who writes "Gent." after his name on the title-page. She had been kind to him in sickness and had "yielded to each look of his a sweet reply." After giving these slight hints, he pushes forth from the moorings of realism and sets sail on the ocean of the sonneteer's fancy, meeting the usual adventures. His sonnets, while showing versatility and ingenuity, lack spontaneous feeling and have serious defects in form; yet these defects are in part offset by their conversational ease and dramatic vividness.

## TO FIDESSA

I

Fertur Fortunam Fortuna favere ferenti

Fidessa fair, long live a happy maiden!
  Blest from thy cradle by a worthy mother,
  High-thoughted like to her, with bounty laden,
  Like pleasing grace affording, one and other;
Sweet model of thy far renowned sire!
  Hold back a while thy ever-giving hand,
  And though these free penned lines do nought require,
  For that they scorn at base reward to stand,
Yet crave they most for that they beg the least
  Dumb is the message of my hidden grief,
  And store of speech by silence is increased;
  O let me die or purchase some relief!
Bounteous Fidessa cannot be so cruel
As for to make my heart her fancy's fuel!

II

How can that piercing crystal-painted eye,
  That gave the onset to my high aspiring.
  Yielding each look of mine a sweet reply,
  Adding new courage to my heart's desiring,
How can it shut itself within her ark,
  And keep herself and me both from the light,
  Making us walk in all misguiding dark,
  Aye to remain in confines of the night?
How is it that so little room contains it,
  That guides the orient as the world the sun,
  Which once obscured most bitterly complains it,
  Because it knows and rules whate'er is done?
The reason is that they may dread her sight,
Who doth both give and take away their light.


III

Venus, and young Adonis sitting by her,
  Under a myrtle shade, began to woo him;
  She told the youngling how god Mars did try her,
  And as he fell to her, so fell she to him.
"Even thus," quoth she, "the wanton god embraced me!"
  And then she clasped Adonis in her arms;
  "Even thus," quoth she, "the warlike god unlaced me!"
  As if the boy should use like loving charms.
But he, a wayward boy, refused the offer,
  And ran away the beauteous queen neglecting
  Showing both folly to abuse her proffer,
  And all his sex of cowardice detecting.
O that I had my mistress at that bay,

To kiss and clip me till I ran away!


### IV

Did you sometimes three German brethren see,
  Rancour 'twixt two of them so raging rife,
  That th' one could stick the other with his knife?
Now if the third assaulted chance to be
By a fourth stranger, him set on the three,
  Them two 'twixt whom afore was deadly strife
  Made one to rob the stranger of his life;
Then do you know our state as well as we.
  Beauty and chastity with her were born,
Both at one birth, and up with her did grow.
  Beauty still foe to chastity was sworn,
And chastity sworn to be beauty's foe;
  And yet when I lay siege unto her heart,
  Beauty and chastity both take her part.


### V

Arraigned, poor captive at the bar I stand,
  The bar of beauty, bar to all my joys;
  And up I hold my ever trembling hand,
  Wishing or life or death to end annoys.
And when the judge doth question of the guilt,
  And bids me speak, then sorrow shuts up words.
  Yea, though he say, "Speak boldly what thou wilt!"
  Yet my confused affects no speech affords,
For why? Alas, my passions have no bound,
  For fear of death that penetrates so near;

And still one grief another doth confound,
Yet doth at length a way to speech appear.
Then, for I speak too late, the Judge doth give
His sentence that in prison I shall live.


VI

Unhappy sentence, worst of worst of pains,
  To be in darksome silence, out of ken,
  Banished from all that bliss the world contains,
  And thrust from out the companies of men!
Unhappy sentence, worse than worst of deaths,
  Never to see Fidessa's lovely face!
  O better were I lose ten thousand breaths,
  Than ever live in such unseen disgrace!
Unhappy sentence, worse than pains of hell,
  To live in self-tormenting griefs alone;
  Having my heart, my prison and my cell,
  And there consumed without relief to moan!
If that the sentence so unhappy be,
Then what am I that gave the same to me?


VII

Oft have mine eyes, the agents of mine heart,
  False traitor eyes conspiring my decay,
  Pleaded for grace with dumb and silent art,
  Streaming forth tears my sorrows to allay;
Moaning the wrong they do unto their lord,
  Forcing the cruel fair by means to yield;
  Making her 'gainst her will some grace t'afford,

    And striving sore at length to win the field;
Thus work they means to feed my fainting hope,
    And strengthened hope adds matter to each thought;
    Yet when they all come to their end and scope
    They do but wholly bring poor me to nought.
She'll never yield although they ever cry,
And therefore we must all together die.


## VIII

Grief-urging guest, great cause have I to plain me,
    Yet hope persuading hope expecteth grace,
    And saith none but myself shall ever pain me;
    But grief my hopes exceedeth in this case;
For still my fortune ever more doth cross me
    By worse events than ever I expected;
    And here and there ten thousand ways doth toss me,
    With sad remembrance of my time neglected.
These breed such thoughts as set my heart on fire,
    And like fell hounds pursue me to my death;
    Traitors unto their sovereign lord and sire,
    Unkind exactors of their father's breath,
Whom in their rage they shall no sooner kill
Than they themselves themselves unjustly spill.


## IX

My spotless love that never yet was tainted,
    My loyal heart that never can be moved,
    My growing hope that never yet hath fainted,
    My constancy that you full well have proved,

All these consented have to plead for grace
  These all lie crying at the door of beauty;--
  This wails, this sends out tears, this cries apace,
  All do reward expect of faith and duty;
Now either thou must prove th' unkindest one,
  And as thou fairest art must cruelest be,
  Or else with pity yield unto their moan,
  Their moan that ever will importune thee.
Ah, thou must be unkind, and give denial,
And I, poor I, must stand unto my trial!


X

Clip not, sweet love, the wings of my desire,
  Although it soar aloft and mount too high:
  But rather bear with me though I aspire,
  For I have wings to bear me to the sky.
What though I mount, there is no sun but thee!
  And sith no other sun, why should I fear?
  Thou wilt not burn me, though thou terrify,
  And though thy brightness do so great appear.
Dear, I seek not to batter down thy glory,
  Nor do I envy that thy hope increaseth;
  O never think thy fame doth make me sorry!
  For thou must live by fame when beauty ceaseth.
Besides, since from one root we both did spring,
Why should not I thy fame and beauty sing?

XI

Winged with sad woes, why doth fair zephyr blow
  Upon my face, the map of discontent?
  Is it to have the weeds of sorrow grow
  So long and thick, that they will ne'er be spent?
No, fondling, no! It is to cool the fire
  Which hot desire within thy breast hath made.
  Check him but once and he will soon retire.
  O but he sorrows brought which cannot fade!
The sorrows that he brought, he took from thee,
  Which fair Fidessa span and thou must wear!
  Yet hath she nothing done of cruelty,
  But for her sake to try what thou wilt bear.
Come, sorrows, come! You are to me assigned;
I'll bear you all, it is Fidessa's mind.


XII

O if my heavenly sighs must prove annoy,
  Which are the sweetest music to my heart,
  Let it suffice I count them as my joy,
  Sweet bitter joy and pleasant painful smart!
For when my breast is clogged with thousand cares,
  That my poor loaded heart is like to break,
  Then every sigh doth question how it fares,
  Seeming to add their strength, which makes me weak;
Yet for they friendly are, I entertain them,
  And they too well are pleased with their host.
  But I, had not Fidessa been, ere now had slain them;
  It's for her cause they live, in her they boast;

They promise help but when they see her face;
They fainting yield, and dare not sue for grace.


XIII

Compare me to the child that plays with fire,
  Or to the fly that dieth in the flame,
  Or to the foolish boy that did aspire
  To touch the glory of high heaven's frame;
Compare me to Leander struggling in the waves,
  Not able to attain his safety's shore,
  Or to the sick that do expect their graves,
  Or to the captive crying evermore;
Compare me to the weeping wounded hart,
  Moaning with tears the period of his life,
  Or to the boar that will not feel the smart,
  When he is stricken with the butcher's knife;
No man to these can fitly me compare;
These live to die, I die to live in care.

XIV

When silent sleep had closed up mine eyes,
  My watchful mind did then begin to muse;
  A thousand pleasing thoughts did then arise,
  That sought by slights their master to abuse.
I saw, O heavenly sight! Fidessa's face,
  And fair dame nature blushing to behold it;
  Now did she laugh, now wink, now smile apace,
  She took me by the hand and fast did hold it;
Sweetly her sweet body did she lay down by me;
  "Alas, poor wretch," quoth she, "great is thy sorrow;

But thou shall comfort find if thou wilt try me.
I hope, sir boy, you'll tell me news to-morrow."
With that, away she went, and I did wake withal;
When ah! my honey thoughts were turned to gall.


XV

Care-charmer sleep! Sweet ease in restless misery!
  The captive's liberty, and his freedom's song!
  Balm of the bruised heart! Man's chief felicity!
  Brother of quiet death, when life is too too long!
A comedy it is, and now an history;
  What is not sleep unto the feeble mind!
  It easeth him that toils and him that's sorry;
  It makes the deaf to hear, to see the blind;
Ungentle sleep, thou helpest all but me!
  For when I sleep my soul is vexed most.
  It is Fidessa that doth master thee;
  If she approach, alas, thy power is lost!
But here she is! See how he runs amain!
I fear at night he will not come again.


XVI

For I have loved long, I crave reward;
  Reward me not unkindly, think on kindness;
  Kindness becometh those of high regard;
  Regard with clemency a poor man's blindness;
Blindness provokes to pity when it crieth;
  It crieth "Give!" Dear lady, shew some pity!
  Pity or let him die that daily dieth;
  Dieth he not oft who often sings this ditty?

This ditty pleaseth me although it choke me;
  Methinks dame Echo weepeth at my moaning,
  Moaning the woes that to complain provoke me.
  Provoke me now no more, but hear my groaning,
Groaning both day and night doth tear my heart,
My heart doth know the cause and triumphs in the smart.


XVII

Sweet stroke,--so might I thrive as I must praise--
  But sweeter hand that gives so sweet a stroke!
  The lute itself is sweetest when she plays.
  But what hear I? A string through fear is broke!
The lute doth shake as if it were afraid.
  O sure some goddess holds it in her hand,
  A heavenly power that oft hath me dismayed,
  Yet such a power as doth in beauty stand!
Cease lute, my ceaseless suit will ne'er be heard!
  Ah, too hard-hearted she that will not hear it!
  If I but think on joy, my joy is marred;
  My grief is great, yet ever must I bear it;
But love 'twixt us will prove a faithful page,
And she will love my sorrows to assuage.


XVIII

O she must love my sorrows to assuage.
  O God, what joy felt I when she did smile,
  Whom killing grief before did cause to rage!
  Beauty is able sorrow to beguile.
Out, traitor absence! thou dost hinder me,

  And mak'st my mistress often to forget,
  Causing me to rail upon her cruelty,
  Whilst thou my suit injuriously dost let;
And again her presence doth astonish me,
  And strikes me dumb as if my sense were gone;
  Oh, is not this a strange perplexity?
  In presence dumb, she hears not absent moan;
Thus absent presence, present absence maketh,
That hearing my poor suit, she it mistaketh.


### XIX

My pain paints out my love in doleful verse,
  The lively glass wherein she may behold it;
  My verse her wrong to me doth still rehearse,
  But so as it lamenteth to unfold it.
Myself with ceaseless tears my harms bewail,
  And her obdurate heart not to be moved;
  Though long-continued woes my senses fail,
  And curse the day, the hour when first I loved.
She takes the glass wherein herself she sees,
  In bloody colours cruelly depainted;
  And her poor prisoner humbly on his knees,
  Pleading for grace, with heart that never fainted.
She breaks the glass; alas, I cannot choose
But grieve that I should so my labour lose!


### XX

Great is the joy that no tongue can express!
  Fair babe new born, how much dost thou delight me!

But what, is mine so great? Yea, no whit less!
  So great that of all woes it doth acquit me.
It's fair Fidessa that this comfort bringeth,
  Who sorry for the wrongs by her procured,
  Delightful tunes of love, of true love singeth,
  Wherewith her too chaste thoughts were ne'er inured.
She loves, she saith, but with a love not blind.
  Her love is counsel that I should not love,
  But upon virtues fix a stayed mind.
  But what! This new-coined love, love doth reprove?
If this be love of which you make such store,
Sweet, love me less, that you may love me more!


## XXI

He that will Caesar be, or else not be--
  Who can aspire to Caesar's bleeding fame,
  Must be of high resolve; but what is he
  That thinks to gain a second Caesar's name?
Whoe'er he be that climbs above his strength,
  And climbeth high, the greater is his fall!
  For though he sit awhile, we see at length,
  His slippery place no firmness hath at all,
Great is his bruise that falleth from on high.
  This warneth me that I should not aspire;
  Examples should prevail; I care not, I!
  I perish must or have what I desire!
This humour doth with mine full well agree
I must Fidessa's be, or else not be!

## XXII

It was of love, ungentle gentle boy!
  That thou didst come and harbour in my breast;
  Not of intent my body to destroy,
  And have my soul, with restless cares opprest.
But sith thy love doth turn unto my pain,
  Return to Greece, sweet lad, where thou wast born.
  Leave me alone my griefs to entertain,
  If thou forsake me, I am less forlorn;
Although alone, yet shall I find more ease.
  Then see thou hie thee hence, or I will chase thee;
  Men highly wronged care not to displease;
  My fortune hangs on thee, thou dost disgrace me,
Yet at thy farewell, play a friendly part;
To make amends, fly to Fidessa's heart.

## XXIII

Fly to her heart, hover about her heart,
With dainty kisses mollify her heart,
Pierce with thy arrows her obdurate heart,
With sweet allurements ever move her heart,
At midday and at midnight touch her heart,
Be lurking closely, nestle about her heart,
With power--thou art a god!--command her heart,
Kindle thy coals of love about her heart,
Yea, even into thyself transform her heart!
Ah, she must love! Be sure thou have her heart;
And I must die if thou have not her heart;
Thy bed if thou rest well, must be her heart;

He hath the best part sure that hath her heart;
What have I not, if I have but her heart!


## XXIV

Striving is past! Ah, I must sink and drown,
  And that in sight of long descried shore!
  I cannot send for aid unto the town,
  All help is vain and I must die therefore.
Then poor distressed caitiff, be resolved
  To leave this earthly dwelling fraught with care;
  Cease will thy woes, thy corpse in earth involved,
  Thou diest for her that will no help prepare.
O see, my case herself doth now behold;
  The casement open is; she seems to speak;--
  But she has gone! O then I dare be bold
  And needs must say she caused my heart to break.
I die before I drown, O heavy case!
It was because I saw my mistress' face.


## XXV

Compare me to Pygmalion with his image sotted,
  For, as was he, even so am I deceived.
  The shadow only is to me allotted,
  The substance hath of substance me bereaved.
Then poor and helpless must I wander still
  In deep laments to pass succeeding days,
  Welt'ring in woes that poor and mighty kill.
  O who is mighty that so soon decays!
The dread Almighty hath appointed so

    The final period of all worldly things.
    Then as in time they come, so must they go;
    Death common is to beggars and to kings
For whither do I run beside my text?
I run to death, for death must be the next.


## XXVI

The silly bird that hastes unto the net,
  And flutters to and fro till she be taken,
  Doth look some food or succour there to get,
  But loseth life, so much is she mistaken.
The foolish fly that fleeth to the flame
  With ceaseless hovering and with restless flight,
  Is burned straight to ashes in the same,
  And finds her death where was her most delight
The proud aspiring boy that needs would pry
  Into the secrets of the highest seat,
  Had some conceit to gain content thereby,
  Or else his folly sure was wondrous great.
These did through folly perish all and die:
And though I know it, even so do I.


## XXVII

Poor worm, poor silly worm, alas, poor beast!
  Fear makes thee hide thy head within the ground,
  Because of creeping things thou art the least,
  Yet every foot gives thee thy mortal wound.
But I, thy fellow worm, am in worse state,
  For thou thy sun enjoyest, but I want mine.

I live in irksome night, O cruel fate!
    My sun will never rise, nor ever shine.
Thus blind of light, mine eyes misguide my feet,
    And baleful darkness makes me still afraid;
    Men mock me when I stumble in the street,
    And wonder how my young sight so decayed.
Yet do I joy in this, even when I fall,
That I shall see again and then see all.


## XXVIII

Well may my soul, immortal and divine,
  That is imprisoned in a lump of clay,
  Breathe out laments until this body pine,
  That from her takes her pleasures all away.
Pine then, thou loathed prison of my life,
  Untoward subject of the least aggrievance!
  O let me die! Mortality is rife;
  Death comes by wounds, by sickness, care, and chance.
O earth, the time will come when I'll resume thee,
  And in thy bosom make my resting-place;
  Then do not unto hardest sentence doom me;
  Yield, yield betimes; I must and will have grace!
Richly shalt thou be entombed, since, for thy grave,
Fidessa, fair Fidessa, thou shalt have!


## XXIX

Earth, take this earth wherein my spirits languish;
  Spirits, leave this earth that doth in griefs retain you;
  Griefs, chase this earth that it may fade with anguish;

Spirits, avoid these furies which do pain you!
O leave your loathsome prison; freedom gain you;
  Your essence is divine; great is your power;
  And yet you moan your wrongs and sore complain you,
  Hoping for joy which fadeth every hour.
O spirits, your prison loathe and freedom gain you;
  The destinies in deep laments have shut you
  Of mortal hate, because they do disdain you,
  And yet of joy that they in prison put you.
Earth, take this earth with thee to be enclosed;
Life is to me, and I to it, opposed!


### XXX

Weep now no more, mine eyes, but be you drowned
  In your own tears, so many years distilled.
  And let her know that at them long hath frowned,
  That you can weep no more although she willed;
This hap her cruelty hath her allotten,
  Who whilom was commandress of each part;
  That now her proper griefs must be forgotten
  By those true outward signs of inward smart.
For how can he that hath not one tear left him,
  Stream out those floods that are due unto her moaning,
  When both of eyes and tears she hath bereft him?
  O yet I'll signify my grief with groaning;
True sighs, true groans shall echo in the air
And say, Fidessa, though most cruel, is most fair!

## XXXI

Tongue, never cease to sing Fidessa's praise;
  Heart, however she deserve conceive the best;
  Eyes, stand amazed to see her beauty's rays;
  Lips, steal one kiss and be for ever blest;
Hands, touch that hand wherein your life is closed;
  Breast, lock up fast in thee thy life's sole treasure;
  Arms, still embrace and never be disclosed;
  Feet, run to her without or pace or measure;
Tongue, heart, eyes, lips, hands, breast, arms, feet,
  Consent to do true homage to your Queen,
  Lovely, fair, gentle, wise, virtuous, sober, sweet,
  Whose like shall never be, hath never been!
O that I were all tongue, her praise to shew;
Then surely my poor heart were freed from woe!

## XXXII

Sore sick of late, nature her due would have,
  Great was my pain where still my mind did rest;
  No hope but heaven, no comfort but my grave,
  Which is of comforts both the last and least;
But on a sudden, the Almighty sent
  Sweet ease to the distressed and comfortless,
  And gave me longer time for to repent,
  With health and strength the foes of feebleness;
Yet I my health no sooner 'gan recover,
  But my old thoughts, though full of cares, retained,
  Made me, as erst, become a wretched lover
  Of her that love and lovers aye disdained.

Then was my pain with ease of pain increased,
And I ne'er sick until my sickness ceased.


### XXXIII

He that would fain Fidessa's image see,
  My face of force may be his looking-glass.
  There is she portrayed and her cruelty,
  Which as a wonder through the world must pass.
But were I dead, she would not be betrayed;
  It's I, that 'gainst my will, shall make it known.
  Her cruelty by me must be bewrayed,
  Or I must hide my head and live alone.
I'll pluck my silver hairs from out my head,
  And wash away the wrinkles of my face;
  Closely immured I'll live as I were dead,
  Before she suffer but the least disgrace.
How can I hide that is already known?
I have been seen and have no face but one.


### XXXIV

Fie pleasure, fie! Thou cloy'st me with delight;
  Sweet thoughts, you kill me if you lower stray!
  O many be the joys of one short night!
  Tush, fancies never can desire allay!
Happy, unhappy thoughts! I think, and have not.
  Pleasure, O pleasing pain! Shows nought avail me!
  Mine own conceit doth glad me, more I crave not;
  Yet wanting substance, woe doth still assail me.
Babies do children please, and shadows fools;

Shows have deceived the wisest many a time.
Ever to want our wish, our courage cools.
The ladder broken, 'tis in vain to climb.
But I must wish, and crave, and seek, and climb;
It's hard if I obtain not grace in time.


XXXV

I have not spent the April of my time,
  The sweet of youth in plotting in the air,
  But do at first adventure seek to climb,
  Whilst flowers of blooming years are green and fair.
I am no leaving of all-withering age,
  I have not suffered many winter lours;
  I feel no storm unless my love do rage,
  And then in grief I spend both days and hours.
This yet doth comfort that my flower lasted
  Until it did approach my sun too near;
  And then, alas, untimely was it blasted,
  So soon as once thy beauty did appear!
But after all, my comfort rests in this,
That for thy sake my youth decayed is.


XXXVI

O let my heart, my body, and my tongue
  Bleed forth the lively streams of faith unfeigned,
  Worship my saint the gods and saints among,
  Praise and extol her fair that me hath pained!
O let the smoke of my suppressed desire,
  Raked up in ashes of my burning breast,

   Break out at length and to the clouds aspire,
     Urging the heavens to afford me rest;
But let my body naturally descend
     Into the bowels of our common mother,
     And to the very centre let it wend,
     When it no lower can, her griefs to smother!
And yet when I so low do buried lie,
Then shall my love ascend unto the sky.


### XXXVII

Fair is my love that feeds among the lilies,
     The lilies growing in that pleasant garden
     Where Cupid's mount, that well beloved hill is,
     And where that little god himself is warden.
See where my love sits in the beds of spices,
     Beset all round with camphor, myrrh, and roses,
     And interlaced with curious devices,
     Which her from all the world apart incloses.
There doth she tune her lute for her delight,
     And with sweet music makes the ground to move;
     Whilst I, poor I, do sit in heavy plight,
     Wailing alone my unrespected love,
Not daring rush into so rare a place,
That gives to her, and she to it, a grace.


### XXXVIII

Was never eye did see my mistress' face,
     Was never ear did hear Fidessa's tongue,
     Was never mind that once did mind her grace,

That ever thought the travail to be long.
When her I see, no creature I behold,
  So plainly say these advocates of love,
  That now do fear and now to speak are bold,
  Trembling apace when they resolve to prove.
These strange effects do show a hidden power,
  A majesty all base attempts reproving,
  That glads or daunts as she doth laugh or lower;
  Surely some goddess harbours in their moving
Who thus my Muse from base attempts hath raised,
Whom thus my Muse beyond compare hath praised.


## XXXIX

My lady's hair is threads of beaten gold,
  Her front the purest crystal eye hath seen,
  Her eyes the brightest stars the heavens hold,
  Her cheeks red roses such as seld have been;
Her pretty lips of red vermillion die,
  Her hand of ivory the purest white,
  Her blush Aurora or the morning sky,
  Her breast displays two silver fountains bright
The spheres her voice, her grace the Graces three:
  Her body is the saint that I adore;
  Her smiles and favours sweet as honey be;
  Her feet fair Thetis praiseth evermore.
But ah, the worst and last is yet behind,
For of a griffon she doth bear the mind!

XL

Injurious Fates, to rob me of my bliss,
  And dispossess my heart of all his hope!
  You ought with just revenge to punish miss,
  For unto you the hearts of men are ope.
Injurious Fates, that hardened have her heart,
  Yet make her face to send out pleasing smiles!
  And both are done but to increase my smart,
  And entertain my love with falsed wiles.
Yet being when she smiles surprised with joy,
  I fain would languish in so sweet a pain,
  Beseeching death my body to destroy,
  Lest on the sudden she should frown again.
When men do wish for death, Fates have no force;
But they, when men would live, have no remorse.


XLI

The prison I am in is thy fair face,
  Wherein my liberty enchained lies;
  My thoughts, the bolts that hold me in the place;
  My food, the pleasing looks of thy fair eyes.
Deep is the prison where I lie enclosed,
  Strong are the bolts that in this cell contain me;
  Sharp is the food necessity imposed,
  When hunger makes me feed on that which pains me.
Yet do I love, embrace, and follow fast,
  That holds, that keeps, that discontents me most;
  And list not break, unlock, or seek to waste
  The place, the bolts, the food, though I be lost;

Better in prison ever to remain,
Than being out to suffer greater pain.


XLII

When never-speaking silence proves a wonder,
  When ever-flying flame at home remaineth,
  When all-concealing night keeps darkness under,
  When men-devouring wrong true glory gaineth,
When soul-tormenting grief agrees with joy,
  When Lucifer foreruns the baleful night,
  When Venus doth forsake her little boy,
  When her untoward boy obtaineth sight,
When Sisyphus doth cease to roll his stone,
  When Otus shaketh off his heavy chain,
  When beauty, queen of pleasure, is alone,
  When love and virtue quiet peace disdain;
When these shall be, and I not be,
Then will Fidessa pity me.


XLIII

Tell me of love, sweet Love, who is thy sire,
  Or if thou mortal or immortal be?
  Some say thou art begotten by desire,
  Nourished with hope, and fed with fantasy,
Engendered by a heavenly goddess' eye,
  Lurking most sweetly in an angel's face.
  Others, that beauty thee doth deify;--
  O sovereign beauty, full of power and grace!--
But I must be absurd all this denying,

Because the fairest fair alive ne'er knew thee.
Now, Cupid, comes thy godhead to the trying;
'Twas she alone--such is her power--that slew me;
She shall be Love, and thou a foolish boy,
Whose virtue proves thy power is but a toy.


XLIV

No choice of change can ever change my mind;
  Choiceless my choice, the choicest choice alive;
  Wonder of women, were she not unkind,
  The pitiless of pity to deprive.
Yet she, the kindest creature of her kind,
  Accuseth me of self-ingratitude,
  And well she may, sith by good proof I find
  Myself had died, had she not helpful stood.
For when my sickness had the upper hand,
  And death began to show his awful face,
  She took great pains my pains for to withstand,
  And eased my heart that was in heavy case.
But cruel now, she scorneth what it craveth;
Unkind in kindness, murdering while she saveth.


XLV

Mine eye bewrays the secrets of my heart,
  My heart unfolds his grief before her face;
  Her face--bewitching pleasure of my smart!--
  Deigns not one look of mercy and of grace.
My guilty eye of murder and of treason,--
  Friendly conspirator of my decay,

Dumb eloquence, the lover's strongest reason!--
Doth weep itself for anger quite away,
And chooseth rather not to be, than be
  Disloyal, by too well discharging duty;
  And being out, joys it no more can see
  The sugared charms of all deceiving beauty.
But, for the other greedily doth eye it,
I pray you tell me, what do I get by it?


XLVI

So soon as peeping Lucifer, Aurora's star,
  The sky with golden periwigs doth spangle;
  So soon as Phoebus gives us light from far,
  So soon as fowler doth the bird entangle;
Soon as the watchful bird, clock of the morn,
  Gives intimation of the day's appearing;
Soon as the jolly hunter winds his horn,
  His speech and voice with custom's echo clearing;
Soon as the hungry lion seeks his prey
  In solitary range of pathless mountains;
  Soon as the passenger sets on his way,
  So soon as beasts resort unto the fountains;
So soon mine eyes their office are discharging,
And I my griefs with greater griefs enlarging.


XLVII

I see, I hear, I feel, I know, I rue
  My fate, my fame, my pain, my loss, my fall,
  Mishap, reproach, disdain, a crown, her hue,

    Cruel, still flying, false, fair, funeral,
To cross, to shame, bewitch, deceive, and kill
    My first proceedings in their flowing bloom.
    My worthless pen fast chained to my will,
    My erring life through an uncertain doom,
My thoughts that yet in lowliness do mount,
    My heart the subject of her tyranny;
    What now remains but her severe account
    Of murder's crying guilt, foul butchery!
She was unhappy in her cradle breath,
That given was to be another's death.


## XLVIII

"Murder! O murder!" I can cry no longer.
    "Murder! O murder!" Is there none to aid me?
    Life feeble is in force, death is much stronger;
    Then let me die that shame may not upbraid me;
Nothing is left me now but shame or death.
    I fear she feareth not foul murder's guilt,
    Nor do I fear to lose a servile breath.
    I know my blood was given to be spilt.
What is this life but maze of countless strays,
    The enemy of true felicity,
    Fitly compared to dreams, to flowers, to plays!
    O life, no life to me, but misery!
Of shame or death, if thou must one,
Make choice of death and both are gone.

## XLIX

My cruel fortunes clouded with a frown,
  Lurk in the bosom of eternal night;
  My climbing thoughts are basely hauled down;
  My best devices prove but after-sight.
Poor outcast of the world's exiled room,
  I live in wilderness of deep lament;
  No hope reserved me but a hopeless tomb,
  When fruitless life and fruitful woes are spent.
Shall Phoebus hinder little stars to shine,
  Or lofty cedar mushrooms leave to grow?
  Sure mighty men at little ones repine,
  The rich is to the poor a common foe.
Fidessa, seeing how the world doth go,
Joineth with fortune in my overthrow.


## L

When I the hooks of pleasure first devoured,
  Which undigested threaten now to choke me,
  Fortune on me her golden graces showered;
  O then delight did to delight provoke me!
Delight, false instrument of my decay,
  Delight, the nothing that doth all things move,
  Made me first wander from the perfect way,
  And fast entangled me in the snares of love.
Then my unhappy happiness at first began,
  Happy in that I loved the fairest fair;
  Unhappily despised, a hapless man;
  Thus joy did triumph, triumph did despair.

My conquest is--which shall the conquest gain?--
Fidessa, author both of joy and pain!


LI

Work, work apace, you blessed sisters three,
  In restless twining of my fatal thread!
  O let your nimble hands at once agree,
  To weave it out and cut it off with speed!
Then shall my vexed and tormented ghost
  Have quiet passage to the Elysian rest,
  And sweetly over death and fortune boast
  In everlasting triumphs with the blest.
But ah, too well I know you have conspired
  A lingering death for him that loatheth life,
  As if with woes he never could be tired.
  For this you hide your all-dividing knife.
One comfort yet the heavens have assigned me;
That I must die and leave my griefs behind me.


LII

It is some comfort to the wronged man,
  The wronger of injustice to upbraid.
  Justly myself herein I comfort can,
  And justly call her an ungrateful maid.
Thus am I pleased to rid myself of crime
  And stop the mouth of all-reporting fame,
  Counting my greatest cross the loss of time
  And all my private grief her public shame.
Ah, but to speak the truth, hence are my cares,

And in this comfort all discomfort resteth;
  My harms I cause her scandal unawares;
  Thus love procures the thing that love detesteth.
For he that views the glasses of my smart
Must need report she hath a flinty heart.


LIII

I was a king of sweet content at least,
  But now from out my kingdom banished;
  I was chief guest at fair dame pleasure's feast,
  But now I am for want of succour famished;
I was a saint and heaven was my rest,
  But now cast down into the lowest hell.
  Vile caitiffs may not live among the blest,
  Nor blessed men amongst cursed caitiffs dwell.
Thus am I made an exile of a king;
  Thus choice of meats to want of food is changed;
  Thus heaven's loss doth hellish torments bring;
  Self crosses make me from myself estranged.
Yet am I still the same but made another;
Then not the same; alas, I am no other!


LIV

If great Apollo offered as a dower
  His burning throne to beauty's excellence;
  If Jove himself came in a golden shower
  Down to the earth to fetch fair Io thence;
If Venus in the curled locks was tied
  Of proud Adonis not of gentle kind;

If Tellus for a shepherd's favour died,
  The favour cruel Love to her assigned;
If Heaven's winged herald Hermes had
  His heart enchanted with a country maid;
  If poor Pygmalion was for beauty mad;
  If gods and men have all for beauty strayed:
I am not then ashamed to be included
'Mongst those that love, and be with love deluded.


LV

O, No, I dare not! O, I may not speak!
  Yes, yes, I dare, I can, I must, I will!
  Then heart, pour forth thy plaints and do not break;
  Let never fancy manly courage kill;
Intreat her mildly, words have pleasing charms
  Of force to move the most obdurate heart,
  To take relenting pity of my harms,
  And with unfeigned tears to wail my smart.
Is she a stock, a block, a stone, a flint?
  Hath she nor ears to hear nor eyes to see?
  If so my cries, my prayers, my tears shall stint!
  Lord! how can lovers so bewitched be!
I took her to be beauty's queen alone;
But now I see she is a senseless stone.


LVI

Is trust betrayed? Doth kindness grow unkind?
  Can beauty both at once give life and kill?
  Shall fortune alter the most constant mind?

Will reason yield unto rebelling will?
Doth fancy purchase praise, and virtue shame?
  May show of goodness lurk in treachery?
  Hath truth unto herself procured blame?
  Must sacred muses suffer misery?
Are women woe to men, traps for their falls?
  Differ their words, their deeds, their looks, their lives?
  Have lovers ever been their tennis balls?
  Be husbands fearful of the chastest wives?
All men do these affirm, and so must I,
Unless Fidessa give to me the lie.


## LVII

Three playfellows--such three were never seen
  In Venus' court--upon a summer's day,
  Met altogether on a pleasant green,
  Intending at some pretty game to play.
They Dian, Cupid, and Fidessa were.
  Their wager, beauty, bow, and cruelty;
  The conqueress the stakes away did bear.
  Whose fortune then was it to win all three?
Fidessa, which doth these as weapons use,
  To make the greatest heart her will obey;
  And yet the most obedient to refuse
  As having power poor lovers to betray.
With these she wounds, she heals, gives life and death;
More power hath none that lives by mortal breath.

## LVIII

O beauty, siren! kept with Circe's rod;
  The fairest good in seem but foulest ill;
  The sweetest plague ordained for man by God,
  The pleasing subject of presumptuous will;
Th' alluring object of unstayed eyes;
  Friended of all, but unto all a foe;
  The dearest thing that any creature buys,
  And vainest too, it serves but for a show;
In seem a heaven, and yet from bliss exiling;
  Paying for truest service nought but pain;
  Young men's undoing, young and old beguiling;
  Man's greatest loss though thought his greatest gain!
True, that all this with pain enough I prove;
And yet most true, I will Fidessa love.

## LIX

Do I unto a cruel tiger play,
  That preys on me as wolf upon the lambs,
  Who fear the danger both of night and day
  And run for succour to their tender dams?
Yet will I pray, though she be ever cruel,
  On bended knee and with submissive heart.
  She is the fire and I must be the fuel;
  She must inflict and I endure the smart.
She must, she shall be mistress of her will,
  And I, poor I, obedient to the same;
  As fit to suffer death as she to kill;
  As ready to be blamed as she to blame.

And for I am the subject of her ire,
All men shall know thereby my love entire.

## LX

O let me sigh, weep, wail, and cry no more;
Or let me sigh, weep, wail, cry more and more!
Yea, let me sigh, weep, wail, cry evermore,
For she doth pity my complaints no more
Than cruel pagan or the savage Moor;
But still doth add unto my torments more,
Which grievous are to me by so much more
As she inflicts them and doth wish them more.
O let thy mercy, merciless, be never more!
So shall sweet death to me be welcome, more
Than is to hungry beasts the grassy moor,
As she that to affliction adds yet more,
Becomes more cruel by still adding more!
Weary am I to speak of this word "more;"
Yet never weary she, to plague me more!

## LXI

Fidessa's worth in time begetteth praise;
  Time, praise; praise, fame; fame, wonderment;
  Wonder, fame, praise, time, her worth do raise
  To highest pitch of dread astonishment.
Yet time in time her hardened heart bewrayeth
  And praise itself her cruelty dispraiseth.
  So that through praise, alas, her praise decayeth,
  And that which makes it fall her honour raiseth!

Most strange, yet true! So wonder, wonder still,
  And follow fast the wonder of these days;
  For well I know all wonder to fulfil
  Her will at length unto my will obeys.
Meantime let others praise her constancy,
And me attend upon her clemency.


## LXII

Most true that I must fair Fidessa love.
Most true that fair Fidessa cannot love.
Most true that I do feel the pains of love.
Most true that I am captive unto love.
Most true that I deluded am with love.
Most true that I do find the sleights of love.
Most true that nothing can procure her love.
Most true that I must perish in my love.
Most true that she contemns the god of love.
Most true that he is snared with her love.
Most true that she would have me cease to love.
Most true that she herself alone is love.
Most true that though she hated, I would love.
Most true that dearest life shall end with love.


## FINIS

Talis apud tales, talis sub tempore tali:
Subque meo tali judice, talis ero.

# CHLORIS
## OR, THE COMPLAINT OF THE PASSIONATE DESPISED SHEPHERD
### by
### WILLIAM SMITH

## WILLIAM SMITH

The sub-title of Chloris arouses an expectation that is gratified in the pastoral modishness of the sonnets. Corin sits under the "lofty pines, co-partners of his woe," with oaten reed at his lips, and calls on sylvans, lambkins and all Parnassans to testify to the beauty and cruelty of Chloris. The attitude is a self-conscious one, yet the poem reveals little of the personality of the author beyond the facts of his youthfulness and of his devotion to "the most excellent and learned Shepheard, Colin Cloute." It was in 1595, but one year before the publication of Chloris, that Spenser had sung his own sonnets of true love, and it is perhaps on this account that William Smith finds him in a mood favourable to the defence of a young aspirant. At any rate, the language of the dedication rings with something more than mere desire for distinguished patronage. The youth looks with a beautiful humility upward toward the greater but "dear and most entire beloved" poet. His own sonnets, he says, are "of my study the budding springs"; they are but "young-hatched orphan things." He nowhere boasts that they will give immortal renown to the scornful beauty, but modestly promises that if her cruel disdain does not ruin him, the time shall come when he "more large" her "praises forth shall pen." Chloris had once been favourable, as sonnet forty-eight distinctly shows, but the cycle does not bring any happy conclusion to the story. Corin is left weeping but faithful, and the picture of Chloris is composed of such faint outlines only as the sonneteer's conventions can delineate. Beyond this no certain information in regard to poet or honoured lady has yet been unearthed.

For all its formality, however, the sonnet-cycle is not wanting in touches of real feeling and lines of musical sweetness; the writer shows considerable skill in the management of rime, and in structure he adopts the form preferred by Shakespeare, whose "sugared sonnets" may by this date have passed beneath his eye. The melodies piped by other sonnet-shepherds re-echo with a great deal of distinctness in Covin's strains; nevertheless he has himself taken a draught from the true Elizabethan fount of lyric inspiration, and the nymph Chloris with her heart-robbing eye well deserves a place on the snow-soft downs where the sonneteering shepherds were wont to assemble.

## TO THE MOST EXCELLENT AND LEARNED SHEPHERD COLIN CLOUT

I

Colin my dear and most entire beloved,
  My muse audacious stoops her pitch to thee,
  Desiring that thy patience be not moved
  By these rude lines, written here you see;
Fain would my muse whom cruel love hath wronged,
  Shroud her love labours under thy protection,
  And I myself with ardent zeal have longed
  That thou mightst know to thee my true affection.
Therefore, good Colin, graciously accept
  A few sad sonnets which my muse hath framed;
  Though they but newly from the shell are crept,
  Suffer them not by envy to be blamed,
But underneath the shadow of thy wings
Give warmth to these young-hatched orphan things.

II

Give warmth to these young-hatched orphan things,
  Which chill with cold to thee for succour creep;
  They of my study are the budding springs;

Longer I cannot them in silence keep.
They will be gadding sore against my mind.
  But courteous shepherd, if they run astray,
  Conduct them that they may the pathway find,
  And teach them how the mean observe they may.
Thou shalt them ken by their discording notes,
  Their weeds are plain, such as poor shepherds wear;
  Unshapen, torn, and ragged are their coats,
  Yet forth they wand'ring are devoid of fear.
They which have tasted of the muses' spring,
I hope will smile upon the tunes they sing.


## TO ALL SHEPHERDS IN GENERAL


You whom the world admires for rarest style,
  You which have sung the sonnets of true love,
  Upon my maiden verse with favour smile,
  Whose weak-penned muse to fly too soon doth prove;
Before her feathers have their full perfection,
She soars aloft, pricked on by blind affection.

You whose deep wits, ingine, and industry,
  The everlasting palm of praise have won,
  You paragons of learned poesy,
  Favour these mists, which fall before your sun,
Intentions leading to a more effect
If you them grace but with your mild aspect.

And thou the Genius of my ill-tuned note,
  Whose beauty urged hath my rustic vein

Through mighty oceans of despair to float,
That I in rime thy cruelty complain:
Vouchsafe to read these lines both harsh and bad
Nuntiates of woe with sorrow being clad.

# CHLORIS

I

Courteous Calliope, vouchsafe to lend
  Thy helping hand to my untuned song,
    And grace these lines which I to write pretend,
    Compelled by love which doth poor Corin wrong.
And those thy sacred sisters I beseech,
  Which on Parnassus' mount do ever dwell,
    To shield my country muse and rural speech
    By their divine authority and spell.
Lastly to thee, O Pan, the shepherds' king,
  And you swift-footed Dryades I call;
    Attend to hear a swain in verse to sing
    Sonnets of her that keeps his heart in thrall!
O Chloris, weigh the task I undertake!
Thy beauty subject of my song I make.

II

Thy beauty subject of my song I make,
  O fairest fair, on whom depends my life!
    Refuse not then the task I undertake,
    To please thy rage and to appease my strife;
But with one smile remunerate my toil,

None other guerdon I of thee desire.
　Give not my lowly muse new-hatched the foil,
　But warmth that she may at the length aspire
Unto the temples of thy star-bright eyes,
　Upon whose round orbs perfect beauty sits,
　From whence such glorious crystal beams arise,
　As best my Chloris' seemly face befits;
Which eyes, which beauty, which bright crystal beam,
Which face of thine hath made my love extreme.


III

Feed, silly sheep, although your keeper pineth,
　Yet like to Tantalus doth see his food.
　Skip you and leap, no bright Apollo shineth,
　Whilst I bewail my sorrows in yon wood,
Where woeful Philomela doth record,
　And sings with notes of sad and dire lament
　The tragedy wrought by her sisters' lord;
　I'll bear a part in her black discontent.
That pipe which erst was wont to make you glee
　Upon these downs whereon you careless graze,
　Shall to her mournful music tuned be.
　Let not my plaints, poor lambkins, you amaze;
There underneath that dark and dusky bower,
Whole showers of tears to Chloris I will pour.

## IV

Whole showers of tears to Chloris I will pour,
  As true oblations of my sincere love,
  If that will not suffice, most fairest flower,
  Then shall my sighs thee unto pity move.
If neither tears nor sighs can aught prevail,
  My streaming blood thine anger shall appease,
  This hand of mine by vigour shall assail
  To tear my heart asunder thee to please.
Celestial powers on you I invocate;
  You know the chaste affections of my mind,
  I never did my faith yet violate;
  Why should my Chloris then be so unkind?
That neither tears, nor sighs, nor streaming blood,
Can unto mercy move her cruel mood.

## V

You fawns and silvans, when my Chloris brings
  Her flocks to water in your pleasant plains,
  Solicit her to pity Corin's strings,
  The smart whereof for her he still sustains.
For she is ruthless of my woeful song;
  My oaten reed she not delights to hear.
  O Chloris, Chloris! Corin thou dost wrong,
  Who loves thee better than his own heart dear.
The flames of Aetna are not half so hot
  As is the fire which thy disdain hath bread.
  Ah cruel fates, why do you then besot
  Poor Corin's soul with love, when love is fled?

Either cause cruel Chloris to relent,
Or let me die upon the wound she sent!

## VI

You lofty pines, co-partners of my woe,
  When Chloris sitteth underneath your shade,
  To her those sighs and tears I pray you show,
  Whilst you attending I for her have made.
Whilst you attending, dropped have sweet balm
  In token that you pity my distress,
  Zephirus hath your stately boughs made calm.
  Whilst I to you my sorrows did express,
The neighbour mountains bended have their tops,
  When they have heard my rueful melody,
  And elves in rings about me leaps and hops,
  To frame my passions to their jollity.
Resounding echoes from their obscure caves,
Reiterate what most my fancy craves.

## VII

What need I mourn, seeing Pan our sacred king
  Was of that nymph fair Syrinx coy disdained?
  The world's great light which comforteth each thing,
  All comfortless for Daphne's sake remained.
If gods can find no help to heal the sore
  Made by love's shafts, which pointed are with fire,
  Unhappy Corin, then thy chance deplore,
  Sith they despair by wanting their desire.
I am not Pan though I a shepherd be,

Yet is my love as fair as Syrinx was.
My songs cannot with Phoebus' tunes agree,
Yet Chloris' doth his Daphne's far surpass.
How much more fair by so much more unkind,
Than Syrinx coy, or Daphne, I her find!

VIII

No sooner had fair Phoebus trimmed his car,
  Being newly risen from Aurora's bed,
  But I in whom despair and hope did war,
  My unpenned flock unto the mountains led.
Tripping upon the snow-soft downs I spied
  Three nymphs more fairer than those beautys three
  Which did appear to Paris on mount Ide.
  Coming more near, my goddess I there see;
For she the field-nymphs oftentimes doth haunt,
  To hunt with them the fierce and savage boar;
  And having sported virelays they chaunt,
  Whilst I unhappy helpless cares deplore.
There did I call to her, ah too unkind!
But tiger-like, of me she had no mind.

IX

Unto the fountain where fair Delia chaste
  The proud Acteon turned to a hart,
  I drove my flock, that water sweet to taste,
  'Cause from the welkin Phoebus 'gan depart.
There did I see the nymph whom I admire,
  Rememb'ring her locks, of which the yellow hue

  Made blush the beauties of her curled wire,
    Which Jove himself with wonder well might view;
  Then red with ire, her tresses she berent,
    And weeping hid the beauty of her face,
    Whilst I amazed at her discontent,
    With tears and sighs do humbly sue for grace;
  But she regarding neither tears nor moan,
  Flies from the fountain leaving me alone.

### X

Am I a Gorgon that she doth me fly,
  Or was I hatched in the river Nile?
  Or doth my Chloris stand in doubt that I
  With syren songs do seek her to beguile?
If any one of these she can object
  'Gainst me, which chaste affected love protest,
  Then might my fortunes by her frowns be checked,
  And blameless she from scandal free might rest.
But seeing I am no hideous monster born,
  But have that shape which other men do bear,
  Which form great Jupiter did never scorn,
  Amongst his subjects here on earth to wear,
Why should she then that soul with sorrow fill,
Which vowed hath to love and serve her still?

### XI

Tell me, my dear, what moves thy ruthless mind
  To be so cruel, seeing thou art so fair?
  Did nature frame thy beauty so unkind?

Or dost thou scorn to pity my despair?
O no, it was not nature's ornament,
  But winged love's unpartial cruel wound,
  Which in my heart is ever permanent,
  Until my Chloris make me whole and sound.
O glorious love-god, think on my heart's grief;
  Let not thy vassal pine through deep disdain;
  By wounding Chloris I shall find relief,
  If thou impart to her some of my pain.
She doth thy temples and thy shrines abject;
They with Amintas' flowers by me are decked.


XII

Cease, eyes, to weep sith none bemoans your weeping;
  Leave off, good muse, to sound the cruel name
  Of my love's queen which hath my heart in keeping,
  Yet of my love doth make a jesting game!
Long hath my sufferance laboured to inforce
  One pearl of pity from her pretty eyes,
  Whilst I with restless oceans of remorse
  Bedew the banks where my fair Chloris lies,
Where my fair Chloris bathes her tender skin,
  And doth triumph to see such rivers fall
  From those moist springs, which never dry have been
  Since she their honour hath detained in thrall;
And still she scorns one favouring smile to show
Unto those waves proceeding from my woe.

XIII

A Dream

What time fair Titan in the zenith sat,
  And equally the fixed poles did heat,
  When to my flock my daily woes I chat,
  And underneath a broad beech took my seat,
The dreaming god which Morpheus poets call,
  Augmenting fuel to my Aetna's fire,
  With sleep possessing my weak senses all,
  In apparitions makes my hopes aspire.
Methought I saw the nymph I would imbrace,
  With arms abroad coming to me for help,
  A lust-led satyr having her in chase
  Which after her about the fields did yelp.
I seeing my love in perplexed plight,
  A sturdy bat from off an oak I reft,
  And with the ravisher continue fight
  Till breathless I upon the earth him left.
Then when my coy nymph saw her breathless foe,
  With kisses kind she gratifies my pain,
  Protesting never rigour more to show.
  Happy was I this good hap to obtain;
But drowsy slumbers flying to their cell,
  My sudden joy converted was to bale;
  My wonted sorrows still with me do dwell.
  I looked round about on hill and dale,
But I could neither my fair Chloris view,
Nor yet the satyr which erstwhile I slew.

XIV

Mournful Amintas, thou didst pine with care,
  Because the fates by their untimely doom
  Of life bereft thy loving Phillis fair,
  When thy love's spring did first begin to bloom.
My care doth countervail that care of thine,
  And yet my Chloris draws her angry breath;
  My hopes still hoping hopeless now repine,
  For living she doth add to me but death.
Thy Phinis, dying, loved thee full dear;
  My Chloris, living, hates poor Corin's love,
  Thus doth my woe as great as thine appear,
  Though sundry accents both our sorrows move.
Thy swan-like songs did show thy dying anguish;
These weeping truce-men show I living languish.


XV

These weeping truce-men show I living languish,
  My woeful wailings tells my discontent;
  Yet Chloris nought esteemeth of mine anguish,
  My thrilling throbs her heart cannot relent.
My kids to hear the rimes and roundelays
  Which I on wasteful hills was wont to sing,
  Did more delight the lark in summer days,
  Whose echo made the neighbour groves to ring.
But now my flock all drooping bleats and cries,
  Because my pipe, the author of their sport,
  All rent and torn and unrespected lies;
  Their lamentations do my cares consort.

They cease to feed and listen to the plaint
Which I pour forth unto a cruel saint.


XVI

Which I pour forth unto a cruel saint,
  Who merciless my prayers doth attend,
  Who tiger-like doth pity my complaint,
  And never ear unto my woes will lend!
But still false hope dispairing life deludes,
  And tells my fancy I shall grace obtain;
  But Chloris fair my orisons concludes
  With fearful frowns, presagers of my pain.
Thus do I spend the weary wand'ring day,
  Oppressed with a chaos of heart's grief;
  Thus I consume the obscure night away,
  Neglecting sleep which brings all cares relief;
Thus do I pass my ling'ring life in woe;
But when my bliss will come I do not know.


XVII

The perils which Leander took in hand
  Fair Hero's love and favour to obtain,
  When void of fear securely leaving land,
  Through Hellespont he swam to Cestos' main,
His dangers should not counterpoise my toil,
  If my dear love would once but pity show,
  To quench these flames which in my breast do broil,
  Or dry these springs which from mine eyes do flow.
Not only Hellespont but ocean seas,

For her sweet sake to ford I would attempt,
So that my travels would her ire appease,
My soul from thrall and languish to exempt.
O what is't not poor I would undertake,
If labour could my peace with Chloris make!


XVIII

My love, I cannot thy rare beauties place
  Under those forms which many writers use:
  Some like to stones compare their mistress' face;
  Some in the name of flowers do love abuse;
Some makes their love a goldsmith's shop to be,
  Where orient pearls and precious stones abound;
  In my conceit these far do disagree
  The perfect praise of beauty forth to sound.
O Chloris, thou dost imitate thyself,
  Self's imitating passeth precious stones,
  Or all the eastern Indian golden pelf;
  Thy red and white with purest fair atones;
Matchless for beauty nature hath thee framed,
Only unkind and cruel thou art named!


XIX

The hound by eating grass doth find relief,
  For being sick it is his choicest meat;
  The wounded hart doth ease his pain and grief
  If he the herb dictamion may eat;
The loathsome snake renews his sight again,
  When he casts off his withered coat and hue;

The sky-bred eagle fresh age doth obtain
When he his beak decayed doth renew.
I worse than these whose sore no salve can cure,
  Whose grief no herb nor plant nor tree can ease;
  Remediless, I still must pain endure,
  Till I my Chloris' furious mood can please;
She like the scorpion gave to me a wound,
And like the scorpion she must make me sound.

## XX

Ye wasteful woods, bear witness of my woe,
  Wherein my plaints did oftentimes abound;
  Ye careless birds my sorrows well do know,
  They in your songs were wont to make a sound!
Thou pleasant spring canst record likewise bear
  Of my designs and sad disparagement,
  When thy transparent billows mingled were
  With those downfalls which from mine eyes were sent!
The echo of my still-lamenting cries,
  From hollow vaults in treble voice resoundeth,
  And then into the empty air it flies,
  And back again from whence it came reboundeth.
That nymph unto my clamors doth reply,
Being likewise scorned in love as well as I.

## XXI

Being likewise scorned in love as well as I
  By that self-loving boy, which did disdain
  To hear her after him for love to cry,

For which in dens obscure she doth remain;
Yet doth she answer to each speech and voice,
  And renders back the last of what we speak,
  But specially, if she might have her choice,
  She of unkindness would her talk forth break.
She loves to hear of love's most sacred name,
  Although, poor nymph, in love she was despised;
  And ever since she hides her head for shame,
  That her true meaning was so lightly prised;
She pitying me, part of my woes doth bear,
As you, good shepherds, listening now shall hear.


## XXII

O fairest fair, to thee I make my plaint,
              (my plaint)
  To thee from whom my cause of grief doth spring;
             (doth spring)
  Attentive be unto the groans, sweet saint,
             (sweet saint)
  Which unto thee in doleful tunes I sing.
             (I sing)
My mournful muse doth always speak of thee;
             (of thee)
  My love is pure, O do it not disdain!
             (disdain)
  With bitter sorrow still oppress not me,
             (not me)
  But mildly look upon me which complain.
             (which complain)
Kill not my true-affecting thoughts, but give
             (but give)

Such precious balm of comfort to my heart,
                    (my heart)
That casting off despair in hope to live,
                    (hope to live)
I may find help at length to ease my smart.
                    (to ease my smart)
So shall you add such courage to my love,
                    (my love)
That fortune false my faith shall not remove.
                    (shall not remove)


## XXIII

The phoenix fair which rich Arabia breeds,
  When wasting time expires her tragedy,
  No more on Phoebus' radiant rays she feeds,
  But heapeth up great store of spicery;
And on a lofty towering cedar tree,
  With heavenly substance she herself consumes,
  From whence she young again appears to be,
  Out of the cinders of her peerless plumes.
So I which long have fried in love's flame,
  The fire not made of spice but sighs and tears,
  Revive again in hope disdain to shame,
  And put to flight the author of my fears.
Her eyes revive decaying life in me,
Though they augmenters of my thraldom be.

## XXIV

Though they augmenters of my thraldom be,
  For her I live and her I love and none else;
  O then, fair eyes, look mildly upon me,
  Who poor, despised, forlorn must live alone else,
And like Amintas haunt the desert cells,
  And moanless there breathe out thy cruelty,
  Where none but care and melancholy dwells.
  I for revenge to Nemesis will cry;
If that will not prevail, my wandering ghost,
  Which breathless here this love-scorched trunk shall leave,
  Shall unto thee with tragic tidings post,
  How thy disdain did life from soul bereave.
Then all too late my death thou wilt repent,
When murther's guilt thy conscience shall torment.


## XXV

Who doth not know that love is triumphant,
  Sitting upon the throne of majesty?
  The gods themselves his cruel darts do daunt,
  And he, blind boy, smiles at their misery.
Love made great Jove ofttimes transform his shape;
  Love made the fierce Alcides stoop at last;
  Achilles, stout and bold, could not escape
  The direful doom which love upon him cast;
Love made Leander pass the dreadful flood
  Which Cestos from Abydos doth divide;
  Love made a chaos where proud Ilion stood,
  Through love the Carthaginian Dido died.

Thus may we see how love doth rule and reigns,
Bringing those under which his power disdains.


### XXVI

Though you be fair and beautiful withal,
  And I am black for which you me despise,
  Know that your beauty subject is to fall,
  Though you esteem it at so high a price.
And time may come when that whereof you boast,
  Which is your youth's chief wealth and ornament,
  Shall withered be by winter's raging frost,
  When beauty's pride and flowering years are spent.
Then wilt thou mourn when none shall thee respect;
  Then wilt thou think how thou hast scorned my tears;
  Then pitiless each one will thee neglect,
  When hoary grey shall dye thy yellow hairs;
Then wilt thou think upon poor Corin's case,
Who loved thee dear, yet lived in thy disgrace.


### XXVII

O Love, leave off with sorrow to torment me;
Let my heart's grief and pining pain content thee!
The breach is made, I give thee leave to enter;
Thee to resist, great god, I dare not venter!
Restless desire doth aggravate mine anguish,
Careful conceits do fill my soul with languish.
Be not too cruel in thy conquest gained,
Thy deadly shafts hath victory obtained;
Batter no more my fort with fierce affection,

But shield me captive under thy protection.
I yield to thee, O Love, thou art the stronger,
Raise then thy siege and trouble me no longer!


XXVIII

What cruel star or fate had domination
  When I was born, that thus my love is crossed?
  Or from what planet had I derivation
  That thus my life in seas of woe is crossed?
Doth any live that ever had such hap
  That all their actions are of none effect,
  Whom fortune never dandled in her lap
  But as an abject still doth me reject?
Ah tickle dame! and yet thou constant art
  My daily grief and anguish to increase,
  And to augment the troubles of my heart
  Thou of these bonds wilt never me release;
So that thy darlings me to be may know
The true idea of all worldly woe.


XXIX

Some in their hearts their mistress' colours bears;
  Some hath her gloves, some other hath her garters,
  Some in a bracelet wears her golden hairs,
  And some with kisses seal their loving charters.
But I which never favour reaped yet,
  Nor had one pleasant look from her fair brow,
  Content myself in silent shade to sit
  In hope at length my cares to overplow.

Meanwhile mine eyes shall feed on her fair face,
  My sighs shall tell to her my sad designs,
  My painful pen shall ever sue for grace
  To help my heart, which languishing now pines;
And I will triumph still amidst my woe
Till mercy shall my sorrows overflow.


## XXX

The raging sea within his limits lies
  And with an ebb his flowing doth discharge;
  The rivers when beyond their bounds they rise,
  Themselves do empty in the ocean large;
But my love's sea which never limit keepeth,
  Which never ebbs but always ever floweth,
  In liquid salt unto my Chloris weepeth,
  Yet frustrate are the tears which he bestoweth.
This sea which first was but a little spring
  Is now so great and far beyond all reason,
  That it a deluge to my thoughts doth bring,
  Which overwhelmed hath my joying season.
So hard and dry is my saint's cruel mind,
These waves no way in her to sink can find.


## XXXI

These waves no way in her to sink can find
  To penetrate the pith of contemplation;
  These tears cannot dissolve her hardened mind,
  Nor move her heart on me to take compassion;
O then, poor Corin, scorned and quite despised,

Loathe now to live since life procures thy woe;
Enough, thou hast thy heart anatomised,
For her sweet sake which will no pity show;
But as cold winter's storms and nipping frost
Can never change sweet Aramanthus' hue,
So though my love and life by her are crossed.
My heart shall still be constant firm and true.
Although Erynnis hinders Hymen's rites,
My fixed faith against oblivion fights.


XXXII

My fixed faith against oblivion fights,
And I cannot forget her, pretty elf,
Although she cruel be unto my plights;
Yet let me rather clean forget myself,
Then her sweet name out of my mind should go,
Which is th' elixir of my pining soul,
From whence the essence of my life doth flow,
Whose beauty rare my senses all control;
Themselves most happy evermore accounting,
That such a nymph is queen of their affection,
With ravished rage they to the skies are mounting,
Esteeming not their thraldom nor subjection;
But still do joy amidst their misery,
With patience bearing love's captivity.


XXXIII

With patience bearing love's captivity,
Themselves unguilty of his wrath alleging;

These homely lines, abjects of poesy,
  For liberty and for their ransom pledging,
And being free they solemnly do vow,
  Under his banner ever arms to bear
  Against those rebels which do disallow
  That love of bliss should be the sovereign heir;
And Chloris if these weeping truce-men may
  One spark of pity from thine eyes obtain,
  In recompense of their sad heavy lay,
  Poor Corin shall thy faithful friend remain;
And what I say I ever will approve,
No joy may be compared to thy love!


XXXIV

The bird of Thrace which doth bewail her rape,
  And murthered Itys eaten by his sire,
  When she her woes in doleful tunes doth shape,
  She sets her breast against a thorny briar;
Because care-charmer sleep should not disturb
  The tragic tale which to the night she tells,
  She doth her rest and quietness thus curb
  Amongst the groves where secret silence dwells:
Even so I wake, and waking wail all night;
  Chloris' unkindness slumbers doth expel;
  I need not thorn's sweet sleep to put to flight,
  Her cruelty my golden rest doth quell,
That day and night to me are always one,
Consumed in woe, in tears, in sighs and moan.

## XXXV

Like to the shipman in his brittle boat.
  Tossed aloft by the unconstant wind,
  By dangerous rocks and whirling gulfs doth float,
  Hoping at length the wished port to find;
So doth my love in stormy billows sail,
  And passeth the gaping Scilla's waves,
  In hope at length with Chloris to prevail
  And win that prize which most my fancy craves,
Which unto me of value will be more
  Then was that rich and wealthy golden fleece.
  Which Jason stout from Colchos' island bore
  With wind in sails unto the shore of Greece.
More rich, more rare, more worth her love I prize
Then all the wealth which under heaven lies.

## XXXVI

O what a wound and what a deadly stroke,
  Doth Cupid give to us perplexed lovers,
  Which cleaves more fast then ivy doth to oak,
  Unto our hearts where he his might discovers!
Though warlike Mars were armed at all points,
  With that tried coat which fiery Vulcan made,
  Love's shafts did penetrate his steeled joints,
  And in his breast in streaming gore did wade.
So pitiless is this fell conqueror
  That in his mother's paps his arrows stuck;
  Such is his rage that he doth not defer
  To wound those orbs from whence he life did suck.

Then sith no mercy he shows to his mother,
We meekly must his force and rigour smother.


## XXXVII

Each beast in field doth wish the morning light;
  The birds to Hesper pleasant lays do sing;
  The wanton kids well-fed rejoice in night,
  Being likewise glad when day begins to spring.
But night nor day are welcome unto me,
  Both can bear witness of my lamentation;
  All day sad sighing Corin you shall see,
  All night he spends in tears and exclamation.
Thus still I live although I take no rest,
  But living look as one that is a-dying;
  Thus my sad soul with care and grief oppressed,
  Seems as a ghost to Styx and Lethe flying.
Thus hath fond love bereft my youthful years
Of all good hap before old age appears.


## XXXVIII

That day wherein mine eyes cannot her see,
  Which is the essence of their crystal sight,
  Both blind, obscure and dim that day they be,
  And are debarred of fair heaven's light;
That day wherein mine ears do want to hear her,
  Hearing that day is from me quite bereft;
  That day wherein to touch I come not near her,
  That day no sense of touching I have left;
That day wherein I lack the fragrant smell,

  Which from her pleasant amber breath proceedeth,
  Smelling that day disdains with me to dwell,
  Only weak hope my pining carcase feedeth.
But burst, poor heart, thou hast no better hope,
Since all thy senses have no further scope!


### XXXIX

The stately lion and the furious bear
  The skill of man doth alter from their kind;
  For where before they wild and savage were,
  By art both tame and meek you shall them find.
The elephant although a mighty beast,
  A man may rule according to his skill;
  The lusty horse obeyeth our behest,
  For with the curb you may him guide at will.
Although the flint most hard contains the fire,
  By force we do his virtue soon obtain,
  For with a steel you shall have your desire,
  Thus man may all things by industry gain;
Only a woman if she list not love,
No art, nor force, can unto pity move.


### XL

No art nor force can unto pity move
  Her stony heart that makes my heart to pant;
  No pleading passions of my extreme love
  Can mollify her mind of adamant.
Ah cruel sex, and foe to all mankind,
  Either you love or else you hate too much!

A glist'ring show of gold in you we find,
And yet you prove but copper in the touch.
But why, O why, do I so far digress?
  Nature you made of pure and fairest mould,
  The pomp and glory of man to depress,
  And as your slaves in thraldom them to hold;
Which by experience now too well I prove,
There is no pain unto the pains of love.


### XLI

Fair shepherdess, when as these rustic lines
  Comes to thy sight, weigh but with what affection
  Thy servile doth depaint his sad designs,
  Which to redress of thee he makes election.
If so you scorn, you kill; if you seem coy,
  You wound poor Corin to the very heart;
  If that you smile, you shall increase his joy;
  If these you like, you banish do all smart.
And this I do protest, most fairest fair,
  My muse shall never cease that hill to climb,
  To which the learned Muses do repair,
  And all to deify thy name in rime;
And never none shall write with truer mind,
As by all proof and trial you shall find.


### XLII

Die, die, my hopes! for you do but augment
  The burning accents of my deep despair;
  Disdain and scorn your downfall do consent;

Tell to the world she is unkind yet fair!
O eyes, close up those ever-running fountains,
  For pitiless are all the tears you shed
    Wherewith you watered have both dales and mountains!
  I see, I see, remorse from her is fled.
Pack hence, ye sighs, into the empty air,
  Into the air that none your sound may hear,
  Sith cruel Chloris hath of you no care,
  Although she once esteemed you full dear!
Let sable night all your disgraces cover,
Yet truer sighs were never sighed by lover.


### XLIII

Thou glorious sun, from whence my lesser light
  The substance of his crystal shine doth borrow,
  Let these my moans find favour in thy sight.
  And with remorse extinguish now my sorrow!
Renew those lamps which thy disdain hath quenched,
  As Phoebus doth his sister Phoebe's shine;
  Consider how thy Corin being drenched
  In seas of woe, to thee his plaints incline,
And at thy feet with tears doth sue for grace,
  Which art the goddess of his chaste desire;
  Let not thy frowns these labours poor deface
  Although aloft they at the first aspire;
And time shall come as yet unknown to men
When I more large thy praises forth shall pen!

## XLIV

When I more large thy praises forth shall show,
  That all the world thy beauty shall admire,
  Desiring that most sacred nymph to know
  Which hath the shepherd's fancy set on fire;
Till then, my dear, let these thine eyes content,
  Till then, fair love, think if I merit favour,
  Till then, O let thy merciful assent
  Relish my hopes with some comforting savour;
So shall you add such courage to my muse
  That she shall climb the steep Parnassus hill,
  That learned poets shall my deeds peruse
  When I from thence obtained have more skill;
And what I sing shall always be of thee
As long as life or breath remains in me!


## XLV

When she was born whom I entirely love,
  Th' immortal gods her birth-rites forth to grace,
  Descending from their glorious seat above,
  They did on her these several virtues place:
First Saturn gave to her sobriety,
  Jove then indued her with comeliness,
  And Sol with wisdom did her beautify,
  Mercury with wit and knowledge did her bless,
Venus with beauty did all parts bedeck,
  Luna therewith did modesty combine,
  Diana chaste all loose desires did check,
  And like a lamp in clearness she doth shine.

But Mars, according to his stubborn kind,
No virtue gave, but a disdainful mind.


XLVI

When Chloris first with her heart-robbing eye
  Inchanted had my silly senses all,
  I little did respect love's cruelty,
  I never thought his snares should me enthrall;
But since her tresses have entangled me,
  My pining flock did never hear me sing
  Those jolly notes which erst did make them glee,
  Nor do my kids about me leap and spring
As they were wont, but when they hear me cry
  They likewise cry and fill the air with bleating;
  Then do my sheep upon the cold earth lie,
  And feed no more, my griefs they are repeating.
O Chloris, if thou then saw'st them and me
I'm sure thou wouldst both pity them and me!


XLVII

I need not tell thee of the lily white,
  Nor of the roseate red which doth thee grace,
  Nor of thy golden hairs like Phoebus bright,
  Nor of the beauty of thy fairest face.
Nor of thine eyes which heavenly stars excel,
  Nor of thine azured veins which are so clear,
  Nor of thy paps where Love himself doth dwell,
  Which like two hills of violets appear.
Nor of thy tender sides, nor belly soft,

Nor of thy goodly thighs as white as snow,
Whose glory to my fancy seemeth oft
That like an arch triumphal they do show.
All these I know that thou dost know too well,
But of thy heart too cruel I thee tell.


XLVIII

But of thy heart too cruel I thee tell,
  Which hath tormented my young budding age,
  And doth, unless your mildness passions quell,
  My utter ruin near at hand presage.
Instead of blood which wont was to display
  His ruddy red upon my hairless face,
  By over-grieving that is fled away,
  Pale dying colour there hath taken place.
Those curled locks which thou wast wont to twist
  Unkempt, unshorn, and out of order been;
  Since my disgrace I had of them no list,
  Since when these eyes no joyful day have seen
Nor never shall till you renew again
The mutual love which did possess us twain.


XLIX

You that embrace enchanting poesy,
  Be gracious to perplexed Corin's lines;
  You that do feel love's proud authority,
  Help me to sing my sighs and sad designs.
Chloris, requite not faithful love with scorn,
  But as thou oughtest have commiseration;

I have enough anatomised and torn
　　　　My heart, thereof to make a pure oblation.
　　Likewise consider how thy Corin prizeth
　　　　Thy parts above each absolute perfection,
　　　　How he of every precious thing deviseth
　　　　To make thee sovereign. Grant me then affection!
　　Else thus I prize thee: Chloris is alone
　　More hard than gold or pearl or precious stone.

www.bookjungle.com  email: sales@bookjungle.com fax: 630-214-0564  mail: Book Jungle  PO Box 2226  Champaign, IL 61825

### The Codes Of Hammurabi And Moses
### W. W. Davies

The discovery of the Hammurabi Code is one of the greatest achievements of archaeology, and is of paramount interest, not only to the student of the Bible, but also to all those interested in ancient history...

**Religion**  **ISBN:** *1-59462-338-4*  **Pages:** 132  **MSRP** *$12.95*  QTY

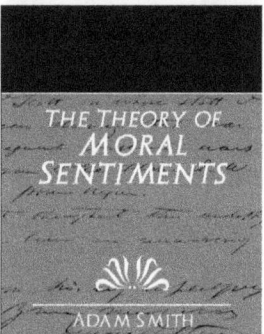

### The Theory of Moral Sentiments
### Adam Smith

This work from 1749. contains original theories of conscience amd moral judgment and it is the foundation for systemof morals.

**Philosophy**  **ISBN:** *1-59462-777-0*  **Pages:** 536  **MSRP** *$19.95*  QTY

### Jessica's First Prayer
### Hesba Stretton

In a screened and secluded corner of one of the many railway-bridges which span the streets of London there could be seen a few years ago, from five o'clock every morning until half past eight, a tidily set-out coffee-stall, consisting of a trestle and board, upon which stood two large tin cans, with a small fire of charcoal burning under each so as to keep the coffee boiling during the early hours of the morning when the work-people were thronging into the city on their way to their daily toil...

**Childrens**  **ISBN:** *1-59462-373-2*  **Pages:** 84  **MSRP** *$9.95*  QTY

### My Life and Work
### Henry Ford

Henry Ford revolutionized the world with his implementation of mass production for the Model T automobile. Gain valuable business insight into his life and work with his own auto-biography... "We have only started on our development of our country we have not as yet, with all our talk of wonderful progress, done more than scratch the surface. The progress has been wonderful enough but..."

**Biographies/**  **ISBN:** *1-59462-198-5*  **Pages:** 300  **MSRP** *$21.95*  QTY

www.bookjungle.com  email: sales@bookjungle.com  fax: 630-214-0564  mail: Book Jungle  PO Box 2226  Champaign, IL 61825

### The Art of Cross-Examination
### Francis Wellman

QTY

I presume it is the experience of every author, after his first book is published upon an important subject, to be almost overwhelmed with a wealth of ideas and illustrations which could readily have been included in his book, and which to his own mind, at least, seem to make a second edition inevitable. Such certainly was the case with me; and when the first edition had reached its sixth impression in five months, I rejoiced to learn that it seemed to my publishers that the book had met with a sufficiently favorable reception to justify a second and considerably enlarged edition. ..

Reference     ISBN: *1-59462-647-2*

Pages:412
MSRP $19.95

### On the Duty of Civil Disobedience
### Henry David Thoreau

QTY

Thoreau wrote his famous essay, On the Duty of Civil Disobedience, as a protest against an unjust but popular war and the immoral but popular institution of slave-owning. He did more than write—he declined to pay his taxes, and was hauled off to gaol in consequence. Who can say how much this refusal of his hastened the end of the war and of slavery ?

Law     ISBN: *1-59462-747-9*

Pages:48
MSRP $7.45

### Dream Psychology Psychoanalysis for Beginners
### Sigmund Freud

QTY

Sigmund Freud, born Sigismund Schlomo Freud (May 6, 1856 - September 23, 1939), was a Jewish-Austrian neurologist and psychiatrist who co-founded the psychoanalytic school of psychology. Freud is best known for his theories of the unconscious mind, especially involving the mechanism of repression; his redefinition of sexual desire as mobile and directed towards a wide variety of objects; and his therapeutic techniques, especially his understanding of transference in the therapeutic relationship and the presumed value of dreams as sources of insight into unconscious desires.

Psychology     ISBN: *1-59462-905-6*

Pages:196
MSRP $15.45

### The Miracle of Right Thought
### Orison Swett Marden

QTY

Believe with all of your heart that you will do what you were made to do. When the mind has once formed the habit of holding cheerful, happy, prosperous pictures, it will not be easy to form the opposite habit. It does not matter how improbable or how far away this realization may see, or how dark the prospects may be, if we visualize them as best we can, as vividly as possible, hold tenaciously to them and vigorously struggle to attain them, they will gradually become actualized, realized in the life. But a desire, a longing without endeavor, a yearning abandoned or held indifferently will vanish without realization.

Self Help     ISBN: *1-59462-644-8*

Pages:360
MSRP $25.45

www.bookjungle.com *email: sales@bookjungle.com fax: 630-214-0564 mail: Book Jungle PO Box 2226 Champaign, IL 61825*

QTY

| | Title | ISBN | Price |
|---|---|---|---|
| ☐ | **The Rosicrucian Cosmo-Conception Mystic Christianity** *by Max Heindel* | ISBN: 1-59462-188-8 | $38.95 |
| | *The Rosicrucian Cosmo-conception is not dogmatic, neither does it appeal to any other authority than the reason of the student. It is: not controversial, but is: sent forth in the, hope that it may help to clear...* | | New Age/Religion Pages 646 |
| ☐ | **Abandonment To Divine Providence** *by Jean-Pierre de Caussade* | ISBN: 1-59462-228-0 | $25.95 |
| | *"The Rev. Jean Pierre de Caussade was one of the most remarkable spiritual writers of the Society of Jesus in France in the 18th Century. His death took place at Toulouse in 1751. His works have gone through many editions and have been republished...* | | Inspirational/Religion Pages 400 |
| ☐ | **Mental Chemistry** *by Charles Haanel* | ISBN: 1-59462-192-6 | $23.95 |
| | *Mental Chemistry allows the change of material conditions by combining and appropriately utilizing the power of the mind. Much like applied chemistry creates something new and unique out of careful combinations of chemicals the mastery of mental chemistry...* | | New Age Pages 354 |
| ☐ | **The Letters of Robert Browning and Elizabeth Barret Barrett 1845-1846 vol II** *by Robert Browning and Elizabeth Barrett* | ISBN: 1-59462-193-4 | $35.95 |
| | | | Biographies Pages 596 |
| ☐ | **Gleanings In Genesis (volume I)** *by Arthur W. Pink* | ISBN: 1-59462-130-6 | $27.45 |
| | *Appropriately has Genesis been termed "the seed plot of the Bible" for in it we have, in germ form, almost all of the great doctrines which are afterwards fully developed in the books of Scripture which follow...* | | Religion/Inspirational Pages 420 |
| ☐ | **The Master Key** *by L. W. de Laurence* | ISBN: 1-59462-001-6 | $30.95 |
| | *In no branch of human knowledge has there been a more lively increase of the spirit of research during the past few years than in the study of Psychology, Concentration and Mental Discipline. The requests for authentic lessons in Thought Control, Mental Discipline and...* | | New Age/Business Pages 422 |
| ☐ | **The Lesser Key Of Solomon Goetia** *by L. W. de Laurence* | ISBN: 1-59462-092-X | $9.95 |
| | *This translation of the first book of the "Lernegton" which is now for the first time made accessible to students of Talismanic Magic was done, after careful collation and edition, from numerous Ancient Manuscripts in Hebrew, Latin, and French...* | | New Age/Occult Pages 92 |
| ☐ | **Rubaiyat Of Omar Khayyam** *by Edward Fitzgerald* | ISBN:1-59462-332-5 | $13.95 |
| | *Edward Fitzgerald, whom the world has already learned, in spite of his own efforts to remain within the shadow of anonymity, to look upon as one of the rarest poets of the century, was born at Bredfield, in Suffolk, on the 31st of March, 1809. He was the third son of John Purcell...* | | Music Pages 172 |
| ☐ | **Ancient Law** *by Henry Maine* | ISBN: 1-59462-128-4 | $29.95 |
| | *The chief object of the following pages is to indicate some of the earliest ideas of mankind, as they are reflected in Ancient Law, and to point out the relation of those ideas to modern thought.* | | Religiom/History Pages 452 |
| ☐ | **Far-Away Stories** *by William J. Locke* | ISBN: 1-59462-129-2 | $19.45 |
| | *"Good wine needs no bush, but a collection of mixed vintages does. And this book is just such a collection. Some of the stories I do not want to remain buried for ever in the museum files of dead magazine-numbers an author's not unpardonable vanity..."* | | Fiction Pages 272 |
| ☐ | **Life of David Crockett** *by David Crockett* | ISBN: 1-59462-250-7 | $27.45 |
| | *"Colonel David Crockett was one of the most remarkable men of the times in which he lived. Born in humble life, but gifted with a strong will, an indomitable courage, and unremitting perseverance...* | | Biographies/New Age Pages 424 |
| ☐ | **Lip-Reading** *by Edward Nitchie* | ISBN: 1-59462-206-X | $25.95 |
| | *Edward B. Nitchie, founder of the New York School for the Hard of Hearing, now the Nitchie School of Lip-Reading, Inc, wrote "LIP-READING Principles and Practice". The development and perfecting of this meritorious work on lip-reading was an undertaking...* | | How-to Pages 400 |
| ☐ | **A Handbook of Suggestive Therapeutics, Applied Hypnotism, Psychic Science** *by Henry Munro* | ISBN: 1-59462-214-0 | $24.95 |
| | | | Health/New Age/Health/Self-help Pages 376 |
| ☐ | **A Doll's House: and Two Other Plays** *by Henrik Ibsen* | ISBN: 1-59462-112-8 | $19.95 |
| | *Henrik Ibsen created this classic when in revolutionary 1848 Rome. Introducing some striking concepts in playwriting for the realist genre, this play has been studied the world over.* | | Fiction/Classics/Plays 308 |
| ☐ | **The Light of Asia** *by sir Edwin Arnold* | ISBN: 1-59462-204-3 | $13.95 |
| | *In this poetic masterpiece, Edwin Arnold describes the life and teachings of Buddha. The man who was to become known as Buddha to the world was born as Prince Gautama of India but he rejected the worldly riches and abandoned the reigns of power when...* | | Religion/History/Biographies Pages 170 |
| ☐ | **The Complete Works of Guy de Maupassant** *by Guy de Maupassant* | ISBN: 1-59462-157-8 | $16.95 |
| | *"For days and days, nights and nights, I had dreamed of that first kiss which was to consecrate our engagement, and I knew not on what spot I should put my lips..."* | | Fiction/Classics Pages 240 |
| ☐ | **The Art of Cross-Examination** *by Francis L. Wellman* | ISBN: 1-59462-309-0 | $26.95 |
| | *Written by a renowned trial lawyer, Wellman imparts his experience and uses case studies to explain how to use psychology to extract desired information through questioning.* | | How-to/Science/Reference Pages 408 |
| ☐ | **Answered or Unanswered?** *by Louisa Vaughan* | ISBN: 1-59462-248-5 | $10.95 |
| | *Miracles of Faith in China* | | Religion Pages 112 |
| ☐ | **The Edinburgh Lectures on Mental Science (1909)** *by Thomas* | ISBN: 1-59462-008-3 | $11.95 |
| | *This book contains the substance of a course of lectures recently given by the writer in the Queen Street Hall, Edinburgh. Its purpose is to indicate the Natural Principles governing the relation between Mental Action and Material Conditions...* | | New Age/Psychology Pages 148 |
| ☐ | **Ayesha** *by H. Rider Haggard* | ISBN: 1-59462-301-5 | $24.95 |
| | *Verily and indeed it is the unexpected that happens! Probably if there was one person upon the earth from whom the Editor of this, and of a certain previous history, did not expect to hear again...* | | Classics Pages 380 |
| ☐ | **Ayala's Angel** *by Anthony Trollope* | ISBN: 1-59462-352-X | $29.95 |
| | *The two girls were both pretty, but Lucy who was twenty-one who supposed to be simple and comparatively unattractive, whereas Ayala was credited, as her Bombwhat romantic name might show, with poetic charm and a taste for romance. Ayala when her father died was nineteen...* | | Fiction Pages 484 |
| ☐ | **The American Commonwealth** *by James Bryce* | ISBN: 1-59462-286-8 | $34.45 |
| | *An interpretation of American democratic political theory. It examines political mechanics and society from the perspective of Scotsman James Bryce* | | Politics Pages 572 |
| ☐ | **Stories of the Pilgrims** *by Margaret P. Pumphrey* | ISBN: 1-59462-116-0 | $17.95 |
| | *This book explores pilgrims religious oppression in England as well as their escape to Holland and eventual crossing to America on the Mayflower, and their early days in New England...* | | History Pages 268 |

www.bookjungle.com  email: sales@bookjungle.com  fax: 630-214-0564  mail: Book Jungle  PO Box 2226  Champaign, IL 61825

| Title | ISBN | Price | QTY |
|---|---|---|---|
| **The Fasting Cure** by *Sinclair Upton* | ISBN: *1-59462-222-1* | $13.95 | |
| In the Cosmopolitan Magazine for May, 1910, and in the Contemporary Review (London) for April, 1910, I published an article dealing with my experiences in fasting. I have written a great many magazine articles, but never one which attracted so much attention... *New Age/Self Help/Health Pages 164* | | | |
| **Hebrew Astrology** by *Sepharial* | ISBN: *1-59462-308-2* | $13.45 | |
| In these days of advanced thinking it is a matter of common observation that we have left many of the old landmarks behind and that we are now pressing forward to greater heights and to a wider horizon than that which represented the mind-content of our progenitors... *Astrology Pages 144* | | | |
| **Thought Vibration or The Law of Attraction in the Thought World** | ISBN: *1-59462-127-6* | $12.95 | |
| by *William Walker Atkinson*    *Psychology/Religion Pages 144* | | | |
| **Optimism** by *Helen Keller* | ISBN: *1-59462-108-X* | $15.95 | |
| Helen Keller was blind, deaf, and mute since 19 months old, yet famously learned how to overcome these handicaps, communicate with the world, and spread her lectures promoting optimism. An inspiring read for everyone... *Biographies/Inspirational Pages 84* | | | |
| **Sara Crewe** by *Frances Burnett* | ISBN: *1-59462-360-0* | $9.45 | |
| In the first place, Miss Minchin lived in London. Her home was a large, dull, tall one, in a large, dull square, where all the houses were alike, and all the sparrows were alike, and where all the door-knockers made the same heavy sound... *Childrens/Classic Pages 88* | | | |
| **The Autobiography of Benjamin Franklin** by *Benjamin Franklin* | ISBN: *1-59462-135-7* | $24.95 | |
| The Autobiography of Benjamin Franklin has probably been more extensively read than any other American historical work, and no other book of its kind has had such ups and downs of fortune. Franklin lived for many years in England, where he was agent... *Biographies/History Pages 332* | | | |

| | |
|---|---|
| **Name** | |
| **Email** | |
| **Telephone** | |
| **Address** | |
| | |
| **City, State ZIP** | |

☐ Credit Card          ☐ Check / Money Order

| | |
|---|---|
| **Credit Card Number** | |
| **Expiration Date** | |
| **Signature** | |

*Please Mail to:*   Book Jungle
                    PO Box 2226
                    Champaign, IL 61825
*or Fax to:*        630-214-0564

### ORDERING INFORMATION

**web**: *www.bookjungle.com*
**email**: *sales@bookjungle.com*
**fax**: *630-214-0564*
**mail**: *Book Jungle  PO Box 2226  Champaign, IL 61825*
**or PayPal** *to sales@bookjungle.com*

*Please contact us for bulk discounts*

### DIRECT-ORDER TERMS

**20% Discount if You Order Two or More Books**
Free Domestic Shipping!
Accepted: Master Card, Visa, Discover, American Express

www.ingramcontent.com/pod-product-compliance
Lightning Source LLC
Chambersburg PA
CBHW080517110426
42742CB00017B/3145